T0156930

21 Days to Happily Ever After

21 Days to Happily Ever After

A Christian Guy's Guide to Being Happily Married

Chris Broughton

iUniverse, Inc.
Bloomington

21 Days to Happily Ever After
A Christian Guy's Guide to Being Happily Married

Copyright © 2012 by Chris Broughton

All rights reserved. No part of this book may be used or reproduced by any means, graphic, electronic, or mechanical, including photocopying, recording, taping or by any information storage retrieval system without the written permission of the publisher except in the case of brief quotations embodied in critical articles and reviews.

iUniverse books may be ordered through booksellers or by contacting:

iUniverse
1663 Liberty Drive
Bloomington, IN 47403
www.iuniverse.com
1-800-Authors (1-800-288-4677)

Because of the dynamic nature of the Internet, any web addresses or links contained in this book may have changed since publication and may no longer be valid. The views expressed in this work are solely those of the author and do not necessarily reflect the views of the publisher, and the publisher hereby disclaims any responsibility for them.

Any people depicted in stock imagery provided by Thinkstock are models, and such images are being used for illustrative purposes only.

Certain stock imagery © Thinkstock.

ISBN: 978-1-4759-4256-9 (sc)
ISBN: 978-1-4759-4258-3 (hc)
ISBN: 978-1-4759-4257-6 (e)

Printed in the United States of America

iUniverse rev. date: 09/04/2012

This work is dedicated to my wife, Gay—my perfect helper, my lover, my one-flesh partner. Thanks for loving me.

Acknowledgments

This work would not have been possible without the help and support of my family and friends, my mentors, and my prayer partners. You have come alongside me and encouraged me. You have held me accountable when I was wandering and have prayed for me when I needed to stand strong.

Thanks be to our Lord and Savior, Jesus Christ, for his constant intercession to the Father on my behalf. He is the source of my strength and happiness. Amen

Section 1

●◆●

Laying the Foundation

I believe in Christianity as I believe that the sun has risen: not only because I see it, but because by it I see everything else.

C. S. Lewis

Chapter 1

•◆•

On your mark, get set, go!

The way to get started is to quit talking and begin doing.
Walt Disney

After more than fifteen years of providing guidance and encouragement to married couples, I have come to the conclusion that no couple wants to be divorced; they simply have not figured out how to live happily ever after. This book is a compilation of lessons I've learned over the last thirty-two years of marriage and fifteen years of ministering to marriages, along with some suggestions for practical application of the lessons. I've written it from my perspective as a husband, as a guide for other husbands. I believe that complete happiness in a marriage requires a husband leading the way, and you can do that by learning and practicing "The Nine Responsibilities of a Husband" presented in section 2 of this book. You will learn the biblical truth about being a provider, lover, warrior, advocate, and intercessor. You will lift high the standard of holiness in your home and lead your family in an atmosphere of forgiveness and reconciliation. A home led by a husband acting on these responsibilities will be filled with peace and happiness and will provide a place for your wife to thrive and be "the wife of noble character" described in Proverbs 31.

This book has twenty-one chapters presented in three sections. Each chapter focuses on a specific aspect of marriage and concludes with guidance for applying what you have learned to your marriage right away. I've purposely kept the chapters short to enable you to get through a chapter each day for twenty-one days—at the end of which you will have developed a set of tools that will move heaven and earth in favor of your marriage. Hear me clearly: this book simply presents opportunities, and you must take advantage of them if you expect to see results. You will begin to live happily ever after only if you choose to work at it.

The wise man in Matthew 7:24–25 built his house on rock so it could stand strong, even when the wind and the rain beat against it. Chapters 2 through 5 will help you establish a similarly solid foundation for your journey to Happily Ever After, with the following rules as building blocks:

- Know you have a relationship with Christ.
- Believe the Holy Bible as the source of truth.
- Understand that God has called you to be a husband in a one-flesh relationship with your wife.

Chapters 6 to 16 present the nine responsibilities of a husband, along with opportunities to practice what God is showing you. As you read them, be encouraged: I have never met an unhappy husband who is acting out these responsibilities.

The chapters in the final third of this book, Chapters 17 to 21, will encourage you to make a difference in your marriage daily, as you apply what you have learned. In doing so you will come to love your wife, lead your family in salvation and forgiveness, and raise the standard of holiness in your home.

The appendix at the end of this book includes some useful documents to help you on your walk to Happily Ever After.

Meet Jim

Jim and I met when he was just about ready to pack it in and give up on his marriage. A construction worker, Jim had been married to Sheila for sixteen years; they had two teenage daughters who kept them busy with sports and school events. A friend of Jim's had advised him to call me for help, so we made an appointment to have lunch together and talk about his situation.

Over lunch we talked about how he and Sheila had met and married, and he bragged about his wonderful daughters. Then, after I felt that I knew a little about his life, I asked him how he and Sheila were doing now. I noticed that when Jim talked about falling in love with and marrying his wife, it was as if he were celebrating his wedding day all over again, and when he described his beautiful daughters, his eyes were full of excitement and a zest for life. But as he began describing the current state of his relationship with Sheila, his sadness showed on his face, and his body language was that of a defeated man. He clearly was not on the road to Happily Ever After.

"I am ready to just leave!" he said, describing his daily battle to make Sheila happy. "I'm worn out with it. No matter what I try, she has a problem with it."

The fighting and arguing between Jim and Sheila had become constant; they seemed never to get along. Jim was 100 percent sure he could not continue to live with the fighting—he had been advised by many of his divorced friends that he should leave the old battle-ax and start living the happy life of a divorced man. I told him divorce was not the answer (Mal. 2:13–16).

As it turns out, Jim was having trouble being happy in several areas of his life. He no longer knew what was important to him—"I'm just not sure what I really want" is how he said it. He had lost his way, and as a result he was feeling confused and sometimes even hopeless.

"Jim, what would you like to see different in your life?" I asked him.

"Oh, that's easy," he said. "I want peace in my house, I want my kids to grow up to be great citizens, and I want to love my wife more fully. But I also want to be able to afford a new V-twin motorcycle with loud exhaust and so much chrome you have to put sunglasses on to even *look* at it."

"Is that all?" I said.

"Yeah," he said. "If only I could just push a button and make that happen." He hung his head a little. "If only," he said again, under his breath.

After meeting with and helping husbands just like Jim for years, I've become convinced of one important fact: no man wants to be divorced; he simply has not learned how to live happily ever after. As I listened to Jim, I recognized a story I'd heard over and over again. So many husbands feel unfulfilled because they are not living as if they are still on their honeymoon, or worse, they are so tired of living like this that they are ready to divorce the woman they once loved. [1]

Current statistics say that 52 percent of marriages end in divorce[2], and more than half the children in America do not have a father figure in their life. This is a tragedy. But it's a tragedy we can do something about, one husband at a time—starting with you.

---

1 The couples mentioned in these pages are all composites of people I have come to know over the years, both personally and through our ministry, Genesis 2:24 Ministries (online at Genesis2-24.net). I've created these composites to illustrate points of interest in this book; any similarity to real people is strictly coincidental.

2 Centers for Disease Control and Prevention, *National Health Statistics Report*, March 22, 2012.

The tools

There are a few tools you will need to gather before we get started. Fortunately, they are simple tools, requiring little space to keep and carry. Kind of like the Pocket Fisherman, only better—because they really, really work.

1) **The first tool is your Bible.** Pick the one you like to read, the one you carry to church. Too often we get tangled up in discussions about whether we should read the King James or the NIV or the New American Amplified with study notes and maps in the back. The important thing is to pick a Bible that you will read and can understand and will carry with you. God is a big boy. He'll make sure he speaks to you through whatever version you choose.

2) **The second tool is a journal.** A journal is a good way to keep track of what God is doing in your life. It doesn't have to be fancy, and you don't have to start every entry with "Dear Diary." If it makes you feel better, call it your "Captain's Log" and start every entry with "Star Date 20100101"—whatever suits you is cool. The point is, a journal needs to be written to you, by you, and for you. If you want to write your journal in some sort of personal shorthand or secret code, or if you want to write it with a crayon on the back of a cereal box, that's fine. Just do it. Your journal will serve to remind you of three important things:

   • where you are
   • where you want to go
   • how God is moving you there

3) **The third tool is "The Nine Responsibilities of a Husband."** They are the meat of section 2 and are listed again in appendix A. If you wish, you can turn to the appendix right now and read through them, but there will be plenty of time for that later.

That's it. That's all you need. No big new toolbox needed. (Of course, if you *want* a new toolbox, please go get one. Because as men, we should all subscribe to this little piece of wisdom from NASCAR driver Richard Hampton: "There is no job so small that you don't need a new tool for it." But I digress …)

Encouragement to run the race

Each chapter of this book will introduce one idea aimed at moving you down the road to Happily Ever After. Each chapter will end with a conclusion and a direction to read, pray, and write in your journal. Be sure to take the time to complete each of these tasks.

Most men lead very busy lives, and many find it hard to fit tasks like these into their daily schedule. I know that the title of this book, *21 Days to Happily Ever After*, implies that you must complete a chapter every day—but before you start, please ask God if that is what he wants you to do. If it takes you sixty days to do the twenty-one days, so be it—but don't skip parts of the book to fit an arbitrary timetable. Read each chapter to get the fundamentals, and answer all the questions to ensure you understand the ideas presented there. Do the assignments; they're not hard, and they won't take all that long. And be sure to document in your journal what you are seeing, hearing, or feeling.

As you progress through the twenty-one chapters, you will begin to see a difference in your relationship with your God and your wife—likely in that order. If you have the courage to embrace your responsibilities, you will be forever changed, and you will indeed live happily ever after. It may be as tough, as exciting, and as rewarding as any two-a-day preseason practice. You may feel sore in places you have not felt before. You may even want to quit partway through, but I encourage you to press on and exercise your God-given ability to fulfill your responsibility as a husband. Your wife will love you for it, our God will reward you for it, and your children and *their* children will be blessed by your actions.

As you progress, be sure to let us know how you are doing. You can join our community at facebook.com/21-days-to-happily-ever-after or contact us directly via our website, Genesis2-24.net/21days.

God bless you and your whole household.

Conclusion

No man wants to be divorced, but no man wants to live unhappily, either. We all have dreams and ambitions and work hard to accomplish them. Be encouraged: God is on your side, and he has provided a way for you to live happily ever after with your wife.

Read … Ephesians 5—the whole chapter. Note that Paul first instructs us to live our lives as Christians, in a way that pleases God. Then he addresses how to live our lives as husbands.

Pray … for the wisdom to discern your goals for your life, your marriage, and your family.

Write … the heading GOALS and today's date at the top of the first page of your journal. Then write at least three goals by completing these sentences:

1) The goal for my life is …
2) The goal for my marriage is …
3) The goal for my family is …

Chapter 2

Taking inventory

You get what you inspect, not what you expect.
W. Edwards Deming

After years of helping men learn how to be happy, I can honestly say that you must have a rock-solid foundation to launch your journey to Happily Ever After. That foundation defines who you are, and it must contain the following basic truths, which will form the bedrock of your walk as a Christian husband:

- The Bible is true, and it is the only source of truth that really matters.
- My name is written in the Lamb's Book of Life, and nothing can take us from God's hand.
- My wife was made by God to be my perfect helper, and my marriage is a covenant relationship.

Knowing where you stand on these three matters is an important step toward being who you are called to be, a husband, and it will guide how you act and react in your marriage.

Meet William

"I am so mad I could spit nails," William said, as soon as I answered the phone.

I paused a second, checked the caller ID to make sure I knew who I was talking to, and said, "Hold on there, slick, what's wrong?"

I heard him exhale angrily. "Cindy promised she would be here in time to help with inventory so we could go out tonight."

William's wife was very involved with a local charity and often ran late. She was sweet, but she had a bad habit of getting talked into helping with projects and forgetting she had promised to help her husband with the small business they owned. She was a hard worker and would definitely get her work done, but too often William felt as if he took second place.

After I had gotten an angry earful, including some choice words unbecoming to the man of God to whom I was speaking, I said, "Let's take a quick inventory before we go further." William knew what was coming next. He didn't like it at first, but he knew it was the right thing to do. So we started the inventory together:

"Are God and the Bible still your source of truth?"

"Yes," he said.

"Is your name in the Lamb's Book of Life?"

"Of course!" he said.

"Is Cindy that perfect helper, sent by God specifically for you, and is your marriage a covenant relationship?"

When William answered, he sounded almost offended. "You know she is," he said. "I love her more than anything … she just makes me mad sometimes."

I continued the inventory by asking, "Are you planning to stay with her forever? Or is this the deal-breaker?"

"That's silly. You know I would never leave her. She means the world to me."

"Great, William," I said. "Now, what was it that was so important that you were ready to spit nails at your perfect helper?"

William and I spent a little time talking about how he could lovingly tell Cindy what he needed rather than unleashing the wrath he had planned. I wanted to help him remember who he is and that the circumstances around him cannot change that. William set his anger aside long enough to inspect the foundation on which he was standing. It was much easier to love his wife when his feet were planted on the rock-steady, biblical foundation built on the assurance that:

- the Bible is true, and it is the only source of truth that really matters;
- his name is in the Lamb's Book of Life, and nothing can take him from God's hand; and
- God made his wife specifically to be his perfect helper.

I happened to have dinner at the same restaurant as William and Cindy later that same night. Judging from the way they were staring into each other's eyes, they must have worked out their differences … and had fun doing it.

How to take inventory

The first thing I teach every husband is how to take an inventory of the foundation on which he stands. I teach him to do this often to prepare him to love his wife no matter the situation or circumstance. You can compare taking inventory to the routine a baseball player goes through when he's getting ready to bat: he'll knock the mud off his cleats, dig the loose dirt out of the batter's box, adjust his helmet and uniform. He makes all these preparations before he swings the bat, because he knows that once the pitcher throws the ball, he will have about half a second to react. Like a batter getting ready to face a 95-mile-per-hour pitch, you need to take inventory of who you are and what you believe before you take action.

The first time you take inventory, you may still be in the process of deciding what you really believe. Don't worry about that. What's more important is that you are honest with the inventory and that you figure out the areas you need to work on. And feel free to take inventory as often as you need to. Just like swinging a bat, the more often you do it, the better you get at it. When I spoke with William, for example, it was likely the tenth time we had taken inventory together—and I have no idea how many times he had asked himself these questions.

The inventory process is really easy. Simply ask yourself the following:

1) *Do I always believe the Bible is true, cover to cover?*
2) *Am I sure that my name is in the Lamb's Book of Life?*
3) *Do I plan to live with my wife no matter what, "until death do us part"?*

Maturing your foundation

You may find that your beliefs will mature and evolve as you take inventory over and over. For example, my belief that the Bible is true was challenged by a health crisis in my family, when my little brother, Clay, was diagnosed with a fatal form of cancer. Satan began to tell me that perhaps the Bible was true only sometimes, because Clay was not getting well despite my prayers for him.

On December 13, 2000—my forty-fifth birthday—Clay called to tell me he was going to the hospital and did not expect to check out again. He was frightened, and he wanted me to come to see him. I jumped in the car and drove the nine hundred miles to where he was. When I arrived, he told me that he was afraid that he had been too bad for God to forgive him—that is what frightened him. We prayed together, and I read him scripture about God's mercy. On December 24 we had communion together. Then my little brother told me he was happy because God had healed him; he was going to go to heaven to claim his new, healed body, and he would see me there later. On December 26 he left this earth and claimed that new body. God reminded me that "to live is Christ and to die is gain" (Phil: 1:22). The healing Clay had wanted was that of his soul; he wanted to be reconciled with God. The Bible was true, and Clay received the desire of his heart.

Because God has helped my foundation mature, I have been a better comfort to my wife as she suffered the loss of both her parents and two older brothers through prolonged illnesses. I can honestly say that taking inventory often has enhanced my ability to be the husband she needs.

The next three chapters will provide more details about the three building blocks of your foundation, one block at a time. Take time for a personal inventory so you can better understand who you are and what you believe. Let God mature that foundation in you and prepare you for your walk as a husband and a man of God.

Conclusion

Taking inventory of who you are and what you believe *before* you take action is an important first step in your journey to Happily Ever After. Begin by asking yourself questions about the three important building blocks necessary for a rock-solid foundation.

Take inventory often, and allow God to mature your foundation. This will make you a better husband.

Read ... Luke 6:48–49. You are called to dig deep and build your foundation on rock.

Pray ... about your foundation. Ask God to help you understand what you truly believe.

Write ... your answers to these three questions:

1) Do I always believe the Bible is true, cover to cover?
2) Am I sure that my name is in the Lamb's Book of Life?
3) Do I plan to live with my wife no matter what, until death do us part?

Write some notes in your journal about what you believe.

Chapter 3

◦ ◆ ◦

Is the Bible true?

All scripture is God-breathed and is valuable for
teaching the truth, convicting of sin, correcting faults
and training in right living; thus anyone who belongs to
God may be fully equipped for every good work.

2 Tim. 3:16–17

very husband experiences life circumstances that will cause
him to react. Some circumstances will seem trivial, such as
being upset in traffic, while others are truly life changing, such as
choosing to pray with your wife. Too often, however, we are taught
to act in a way that does not align with what the Bible tells us is right.
Consider how worldly wisdom differs from scriptural wisdom:

- The world says that we should seek judgment against
  someone who has offended us. The Bible tells us to love our
  neighbor and to give him the shirt off our back when he asks
  for our coat (Luke 6:29).

- The world would tell you that 10 percent of your income is too much to give to the church. God says you are thief if you give anything less (Mal. 3:9–10).
- The world teaches us that some situations are impossible. The Bible tells us that if we speak to a mountain without doubt in our hearts, it will cast itself into the sea (Mark 11:23).

There are countless advice columns and self-help books published every day in America claiming to have the answer to all your problems—and often their ideas are good and their suggestions helpful. But any advice you receive counter to *the* Truth of the Bible must be ignored completely, no matter how good it sounds. Any actions taken without consideration of that Truth will provide poor results at best, and a disaster at worst.

Laying a foundation that's true and square

Our first home was a thousand-square-foot block house in Jacksonville, Florida. It was built "off-grade," which means it sat on a bunch of concrete block piers hidden in a dark, damp crawl space. Sometime before we bought this fixer-upper, some of the piers had shifted, and the floors were so out of level that if you set a ball on the living room floor, it would roll down the hall, past the bathroom, and into the bedroom, picking up speed all along the way.

Pete, a friend of mine who is a tile setter, offered to remodel our bathroom as a housewarming gift. He showed up with all the standard tools, including a six-foot level and various squares and tape measures. Halfway through the job, he carried all those tools to the front porch, threw them into the yard, and said, "I give up." Then he lit a cigarette, sat down on an overturned five-gallon bucket, and just shook his head.

"Chris, there isn't a single square thing in there for me to line up on," he said. "I give up … I'll just have to guess."

Pete and I had been friends since junior high, and I had never seen him that upset. The matter seemed petty to me because I didn't understand all the logistics of the job—and in the end the new tile looked wonderful. But later I came to understand that he was frustrated because his best work could only be "pretty good" with no source of true and square. My crooked house forced Pete to establish "square" based on a foundation that had moved; he knew that if it had moved before, it might move again, and his work would be ruined.

Jesus taught us to use *the* Truth of the Bible to lay a proper foundation for our lives so that we can stand, no matter what happens (Luke 6:49). All men should spend time reading the Bible so that they are equipped for "every good work."

Setting and following a standard

Standards are all around us, and we happily use them. Two pounds of meat is the same amount no matter what store I go to. I can depend on a gallon of gas being a gallon of gas no matter where I pump it. These are things that can be measured, and we have all agreed on how to measure them. No one carries his own scale to the grocery store to see if the butcher has cheated him. And I'll bet no one has ever asked the clerk at the gas station to prove that the pump really dispensed 10 gallons and not 9.8. Why not? Because we understand the standard units of measure and we trust the devices being used to measure them.

When a mason lays bricks, which cannot be moved after they are laid, he uses a level to strike a line to follow. Airline pilots rely on their navigation instruments, not their instincts, so they don't bump into one another (or the ground). And I would much rather use my GPS to find my way out of the woods than guess and continue wandering.

Of course, we can also be tricked by what we *think* is a standard. For example, my wife noticed that the price of the dog food we normally buy had gone down a bit since she last bought it. That seemed like a good deal to her until she got home and realized that the old price was for twenty pounds of food, while the new price was for eighteen pounds, but at a slightly higher price per pound. In both cases she had purchased a "bag" of food. Had she been cheated? She thought so; she had been tricked by the manufacturer to use "bag" rather than "pound" as the standard.

As a man of God, you are to use the Holy Bible as the standard by which you measure your life decisions, big and small. Using the Bible as your standard will lead to a happy and fruitful life. God says it like this: "For I know the plans I have for you, a plan for your well-being, not bad things; a plan to give you a hope and a future" (Jer. 29:11).

Using the Bible to measure what is true can be as simple as doing what it says, without question. Here are some examples:

- Malachi 2:16 tells us that God hates divorce. Do you hate it, too?
- Matthew 6 says that we are to pray for the same forgiveness that we provide. Do you forgive, or are you not forgiven?
- Titus 3:1 tells us to submit to government officials—yet I see plenty of speeding cars sporting magnetic fish symbols. Clearly these drivers are ignoring what the government (and the Bible) has told us to do.

There are certain facts, and that's that

There are certain facts in nature, and that's that. Ignorance of the facts will not keep the laws of nature from affecting you. On the contrary, knowing the laws will make your life easier.

For example, I do not fully understand gravity beyond the fact that it is what keeps me from flying off the earth into space. I know that if I jump off a building, I will eventually hit the ground (ouch).

I know that there is no way around gravity; it is always there, and it always acts the same way. A baby does not understand this fact and will walk right off the top step and tumble down the stairs. That's why we have baby gates. Ignorance of facts does not make you immune to them.

I read a bumper sticker once that said, "God says it, I believe it, that settles it." Good saying; bad theology. If God says it, that settles it. The Bible is full of facts that will affect our lives whether or not we understand or believe them. Knowing the facts can help us avoid tumbling down the stairs just to learn how gravity works—or losing a good friend because we did not understand the power of forgiveness and reconciliation. It is important to read your Bible, but it is more important to accept what it says as fact.

Where do I start?

The Bible is divided into two testaments and sixty-six books. It takes me at least a year to read it through. I understand, therefore, that asking you to read and accept all the facts in the Bible at once is not realistic. So where do you start?

There is no wrong way to read your Bible; God will bless you with understanding when you invest the time to do so. But here are a couple of ideas that might help you get started:

- Throughout this book I use the Bible as the measuring rod for truth, and I've included lots of scriptural references to support the ideas I've presented. Take the time to read these passages, pray about them, and let God help you understand them.

- The Book of Proverbs is full of advice and truths about how to live your life. As a matter of fact, Proverbs 1:1 says that the Proverbs are "about wisdom." I find reading one of these a day enhances my understanding of the facts about

God's world. There are thirty-one Proverbs—one for each day of the month. So on May 1 read Proverbs 1, on May 2 read Proverbs 2, and so on. When June 1 comes along, start over again.

- God is "the alpha and the omega"—the beginning and the end. When asked which books of the Bible best summarize the truth about God and his plan, I always suggest reading Genesis and Revelation, the first and last books of the Bible.

Conclusion

It is important that we base all our life decisions on a clear understanding of what is true and what is not. The laws of nature will always affect us—we just need to know how. Biblical law is similarly intractable. Simply put, the Bible is true, and any knowledge or experience that contradicts the truth according to the Bible is wrong. If you order your marriage according to that Truth, you'll be happy. If you don't, it's just a crapshoot.

Read … Romans 12:1–2. God is calling us to be transformed by his standard, not the world's. With biblical wisdom, we can understand and agree with what God wants.

Pray … for wisdom. Ask God to reveal to you the truth of the Holy Bible and provide you with the strength to avoid worldly standards.

Write … at least two questions you have been pondering. Give full details: what you want to know, why you want to know it, and how this knowledge will affect your life.

Chapter 4

Is my name in the Lamb's Book of Life?

However, do not rejoice that the spirits submit to you,
but rejoice that your names are written in heaven.

Luke 10:20

The scripture above is at the conclusion of a great story of evangelism. Jesus had trained a bunch of regular guys and sent them out to minister in the name of the Father. They came back with all sorts of great stories. They had prayed for people and seen them healed right before their eyes. They had ordered Satan to flee, and the demons obeyed them. They had walked into cities where they were not normally welcome and had been greeted like rock stars. They were feeling like real supermen. But Jesus reminded them of the most important fact they needed to know: they were saved by grace because they were called by his name, not because of what they had or had not done.

Through this message to his disciples, Jesus is speaking to us in plain talk about being saved. That is what is most important in life, he says, no matter what your current life experience. He made sure his disciples understood this important fact, because they needed to tell others.

You may be asking why this salvation story fits into a book about living happily ever after with your wife. There are two important reasons:

1) Jesus said we are to rejoice in our salvation.
2) Couples who have a solid relationship with Christ do not have marital problems. That statement is true 100 percent of the time.

Jesus said it was important

Jesus told his chosen twelve that having their name written in the Book of Life was more important than the ministry from which they had just returned. And in Luke 10:19, Jesus tells his apostles that he has given them authority to trample down all enemy forces—that they are undefeatable—but that they should rejoice because their names are in the Book of Life. Not only does he tell them to rejoice, but he implies that salvation is the *only* thing to get really jazzed about.

I can't imagine their emotions at that moment, but I'll bet they were happy. After all, they had seen a vision of heaven on Earth; no one would be sick anymore, they would be able to feed the hungry, and they would get to hang out with the guy who created the universe. They were on top of their game. This was better than the day their kids were born or the day they caught the biggest bass of anyone in the tournament. They were hitting a home run each time at bat, a hole in one on a par five. They were "badder than Shaft, Super Fly, James Bond, and Kung Fu, all hooked together" (with apologies to ZZ Top's Dusty Hill).

But Jesus wants us to keep our eyes on the prize. Be happy your name is in the Book of Life, he said. If you are saved, you are not of this world, but a citizen of heaven—and you are to rejoice in this important fact.

A 100 percent statistic

When my wife, Gay, and I first met with Robert and Ruth, I asked, "How is your relationship with Christ?"

They began describing their church life and the many committees they were on, until I gently interrupted. "Robert," I said, "tell me about your personal relationship with Jesus Christ."

"Oh, I was saved when I was in grade school," he said, and Ruth chimed in with, "Me, too."

"If a couple is having trouble in their married relationship," Gay said, "one or both of them is having trouble with their relationship with Christ."

Robert objected rather loudly with, "Well, it's not me—I'm fine. It must be her. My life would be just fine if she would behave differently." He was so angry that I thought he was going to hit Gay—until he realized that his anger and accusations had just revealed a deficiency in his relationship with both Christ and his wife. He calmed down and became rather embarrassed.

Again, from my experience, any time there is trouble in a marriage, one or both parties are having trouble with their relationship with Christ. My wife and I have been helping other couples for nearly fifteen years now, and we have never seen a marriage that did not improve when the individuals came into a closer relationship with Christ. As a husband and his wife grow closer to Christ individually, they also grow closer to each other.

You may think that a couple could rally around anything. A hobby, children, or other common interests create wonderful opportunities to come together. But only a relationship with Christ will be everlasting, unchanging, and of eternal value. Remember—it was Jesus himself who told us to rejoice about our relationship with the Father through him.

Conclusion

Jesus told us that our name in his Book of Life was something to celebrate, and that rejoicing in this fact is more important than any other work we do here on earth. One hundred percent of the time, when couples are having trouble in their marriage, one or both of them are having trouble with their relationship with Jesus. You will struggle to succeed in your marriage if you do not have this personal relationship with the risen savior.

Read ... Revelation 3:5. Rejoice that Jesus will be on your side when battles come, and that he will come before God the Father on your behalf.

Pray ... "Lord Jesus, I believe you are the Son of God. Thank you for dying on the cross for my sins. Please forgive my sins and give me the gift of eternal life. I invite you into my life and heart to be my Lord and Savior. I want to serve you always."

Write ... "Today it is settled: no matter what anyone says, I am not going to hell, and no one, not even Satan, can change that. My God is for me, and if God is for me, none can stand against me. I will love like my savior loved me. I am victorious!" Then date your journal entry.

Chapter 5

God made me to be a husband!

*The Lord God took the man and put him in the
Garden of Eden to work it and take care of it.*

Gen. 2:15

The very word *husband* is derived from the Nordic *husdondi,*
which means "the freeholder of a house" (*hus*)—in other
words, the one who tills and cares for the land he owns.

The first book of the Bible states that God created man and
placed him in the garden as its caretaker (Gen. 2:15). He created
us to care for his creation and to have fellowship with him. Just as
the law of gravity explains why what goes up must come down, this
simple biblical dynamic explains why men want to get things done:
we were created to "take care of business."

You were never meant to be alone
Of course, Genesis 2:15 is not the end of the creation story. God
knew man needed a "helper suitable" if he was to succeed in his

mission as the steward of all creation. God says so himself in Genesis 2:18: "It is not good for man to be alone. I will make for him a helper suitable for him." Wow—God said something was "not good." I think I'll listen to that! Because remember, if God says it, that settles it. When God speaks, you know it must be true. This would be a good time to open your Bible and highlight that verse. *God himself* wants man to have help, and that help is woman.

God went all over creation, finding animals and bringing them to Adam. He wanted to see if a dog, a horse, a parrot, or even an elephant might be that one perfect helper for man. Note the level of authority man was given over God's creation. As God and man searched all of creation for a helper, whatever Adam called something became its name. But in all of vast creation, no suitable helper was found—so God created woman (Gen. 2:20–22).

Being a husband is a boys-only club

Remember what you learned in school about the Y chromosome? It is always—and only—passed from father to son. Our Father in heaven passed it to Adam, and it has been passed down from Adam through our forefathers to each of us. Nothing has changed. God cares for husbands so that they can care for their wives. So who are you? You are a husband.

And why are you here? You are here to be a caretaker, a steward for the Father over all his creation. If you are married, your wife is one of those wonderful blessings over which God has given you stewardship. So take care of her; make her prosperous. Woman is the last and best thing God created, and your wife was created especially for you.

Being a husband is forever

When God performed the first wedding, as recounted in Genesis 2:24, he pronounced Adam and Eve man and wife with these words of blessing: "This is why a man is to leave his father and mother and stick with his wife, and they are to be one flesh." God had finished his creation and set into motion the perfect relationship, marriage, and he meant this relationship to be a covenant between two people who become one. As Jesus later said, "No one should split apart what God has joined together" (Matt. 19:6).

A covenant marriage is the only kind of marriage God invented. There are no loopholes that allow you to divorce without sin. This means that divorce is not an option—period! Our society has taught us that if things don't work out, we can dump our current wife and get a new one. But that is not God's plan. This does not mean that there will not be troubles or rocky times in any marriage; it just means that divorce is not the answer to those problems.

Guys, let me be completely honest: when God welds a man and a woman together to form a one-flesh marriage, there is always heat. I mean that in two ways. There is the passion of love that only a man and his wife can know ... I'll call that rubbing each other the right way. There is at least the same level of heat when spouses rub each other the wrong way. When Gay and I rub each other the wrong way—an event that's rare but does occur—we can set the house on fire. But we've made the decision never to divorce, so there is no way out of that burning house. Rather than die in a raging fire; we work on putting the fire out.

There is no deal-breaker in my marriage—nothing Gay can do, say, or think that will make me walk away. My relationship with her is not based on her performance, her looks, or anything she does for me. My marriage is based on the biblical truth that we have become one and that no one should split apart what God has put together.

Conclusion

God invented marriage as a part of his creation story, when he gave man (Adam) stewardship of all creation but realized he needed a helper. God created woman as that helper and caused them to become one flesh through marriage, a covenant relationship meant to last forever.

Read ... Genesis 2:7–25.

Pray ... Each year on my wife's birthday, I make sure to thank God for the miracle of her creation. I pray aloud, "Thank you for the miracle of this woman you created on [her birth date]." I am not sure Gay has ever heard this prayer, but I know that God blesses her through it. Try a similar prayer right now to tell God how much you appreciate his work on the day of your wife's birth.

Write ... Perhaps God is helping you see your wife in a whole new light right now. Take some notes about who she is and why she is exactly what you need.

Section 2

•━◆━•

The Nine Responsibilities of a Husband

Don't judge each day by the harvest you reap
but by the seeds that you plant.

Robert Louis Stevenson

Chapter 6

• ◆ •

Responsibilities of a Husband

Husbands, love your wives, just as Christ loved the church.

Eph. 5:25

The Father's approval

When Gay and I decided to marry, I had to meet with her dad and seek his approval. He wanted to know the usual stuff, like what I planned to do for a living and how I would treat Gay after we were married. Gay was the only girl in the family, the youngest of six—and the apple of her daddy's eye. The wedding happened, and Bruce reluctantly allowed me to take his only daughter to my house as my wife.

Less than a year later, I graduated from college and we moved eight hundred miles away to Florida for my first teaching job. That next Christmas, we traveled back home to Indiana to see her folks. As soon as we arrived at her parent's house, Bruce came outside, held his little girl at arm's length, and said, "Oh, thank God you're well." Later I realized what he was really saying: "I was not sure this boy would step up to his responsibilities and take care of you, but you don't look worse for the wear." My relationship with my father-in-law jumped to a whole new level that day. I had done as I'd promised—I had taken care of his little girl.

When God created your wife, he first placed her in the care of her father, knowing that one day there would be a man to call her his own perfect helper and wife. To make sure that you know your responsibilities as a husband, God has mapped them out in his Word. Remember, your wife is the apple of God's eye; she is his baby girl. Someday God will take her in his arms and know how well you did with your responsibilities as her husband.

God's design for marriage

God designed marriage and presided over the first wedding (Gen. 2:22). He wanted man and woman to live happily ever after in the garden he had created for them, and he knew that their happiness would come from fulfilling their responsibilities as husband and wife. The husband's responsibilities included subduing the earth and ruling over it (Gen. 2:28–30) and never eating from the tree of the knowledge of good and evil (Gen. 2:17).

After the fall, Jesus came to provide a new example for husbands. He didn't just tell us what to do; he set an example for us to follow (Eph. 5:25). He said we are called to love our wives as he loved the church, his bride. He said we should love her as we love ourselves; we must love her so much that we can overlook her imperfections, spots or wrinkles, and set her apart as the object of our love. Jesus took his responsibility as husband to the church very seriously—so much so that at his darkest hour, he prayed so earnestly that his sweat became like drops of blood. Even though it was difficult, he wanted to do his Father's will for his bride (Luke 22:42–44). In Jesus's example we can find the nine responsibilities of a husband.

The nine responsibilities of a husband

The following nine chapters describe those responsibilities. They are presented one at a time, because they have too much substance to absorb in one bite. They are not presented in order of importance—they are equally important. Some will come easy to you; others may not. Be sure to take the time to read the scriptures associated with each one and record what God is telling you about it in your journal.

When Gay and I were first married, I did not fully understand my responsibilities as a husband, nor was I equipped to fulfill them. I knew that I needed to earn a living so we could eat, and I hoped to have a house and a car. I wanted to be sure we went on vacation, and I enjoyed keeping my wife safe. But I did not understand how to pray for her or even love her fully. Worse, I didn't understand how to forgive her. I was a lousy spiritual guide because my relationship with Christ was so weak. I did not have the ability to respond properly to my responsibilities.

Response ability

Gay and I have been married for more than thirty years now, and over the course of those three decades I have learned a number of important lessons. The most important lesson is this: On my own, my ability to respond is extremely limited. With the help of the Holy Spirit, my ability to respond is unlimited.

I want you to learn two important things from this life lesson:

1) You are limited. You cannot respond to your responsibilities as a husband alone. This is not a put-down or a condemnation—it is simply a fact of life. When scripture tells us that we can do all things through Christ who strengthens us (Phil. 4:13), it is also telling us that without him we can do nothing.

2) Jesus told us we will receive power and understanding when the Holy Spirit comes upon us (Acts 1:4–8).

As a husband, it is important that you respond with the ability provided by God through your relationship with Jesus Christ. God will not force you to fulfill your responsibilities as a husband, because forced obedience is simply slavery, and he has called us to freedom. But if you take time to practice your responsibilities, you will please the Father. The fruit of your labor will be a joyful relationship with your wife and peace in your home, and living happily ever after will become the order of the day.

Conclusion

God has mapped out our responsibilities as husbands, but he also has promised to help us with that walk. He asks us to respond to circumstances according to his direction, not advice or information from other sources.

Read ... the nine responsibilities of a husband in the appendix.

Pray ... for strength from the Holy Spirit as you continue on your journey to Happily Ever After.

Write ... As you pray, listen for direction from the Holy Spirit about how to fulfill your responsibilities as a husband. What is God telling you?

Chapter 7

Leader

As a husband, you are to spend time with God in order to know his vision for you and your family (Exod. 33:7–11). You are to cast a vision for focused action serving God (Josh. 3:9–11). You have final **leadership** responsibility for your family (Josh. 24:15). You are the chief priest (Heb. 6:19–20), and you should **lead** your family to victory through salvation, love, forgiveness, and reconciliation (Luke 19:9–10).

Clifford and Debbie

Clifford and Debbie were high school sweethearts who married right out of high school. They both worked physically demanding jobs, so caring for all the household tasks could really wear them down. They also had two preteens at home, and disciplining them had become a source of irritation between them.

"These kids just don't want to mind me," Clifford complained.

"They mind me no matter what I ask of them," Debbie bragged.

"That's because you use that little paddle on them," Clifford said.

Debbie and Clifford had agreed that corporal punishment was okay, but for some reason Debbie never allowed Clifford to administer it. She said she was afraid he would hit them too hard or paddle them when he was still angry. In fact, Debbie often intervened when Clifford was correcting the kids, which made him look as if he had no authority at all.

Gay asked Debbie, "Do you understand that you have made it impossible for Clifford to lead in his home? Don't you *want* your man to lead?"

"Yes, I want him to," Debbie said, "but I'm not sure where he wants to lead us or where he is getting his direction from."

This hurt Clifford and even made him angry, but he simply did not know what to tell Debbie. He admittedly did not have a plan and was not sure how to create one.

I began meeting with Clifford individually to help him write down his vision for his wife and family. During our conversations I would ask him things like, "Where do you see you and Debbie in ten years?" or, "Have you thought about whether you want your kids to go to college?" More often than not, he would answer, "I don't know."

Husbands, you are called to lead—and you can't do that if you are just wandering around. Too many men are afraid to pick a direction for their family because they are worried they will fail trying to get there. Well, going nowhere because you could not decide to go somewhere is failure in itself. Or as revivalist Smith Wigglesworth said, "If you are in the same place today as you were yesterday, you are backsliding."

Be sure you are going somewhere worth going

If you're leading and no one is following, you're just taking a walk.
John Maxwell

Have you ever read the believer's hall of fame in Hebrews 11? It is a wonderful list of men who listened to God and followed him where he led. The men mentioned there often weren't even sure where they were going. Noah built an ark without even knowing what rain was—he just did what God called him to do, and his wife and sons followed. Abraham trusted God and took his first son up on a mountain to sacrifice him, not sure what God was going to do. His son followed him up the mountain, carried the wood for the fire, and even allowed his father to tie him to an altar. Enoch walked so close to God that he just followed him home one day.

Husbands should fix their direction on God's righteousness. Once you have that right, Jesus promised, everything else will be added to you (Matt. 6:33). I believe Noah's sons helped him build the ark not because they understood what God was going to do, but because they were following a man they knew trusted God. Does your wife know that you trust God? Do your kids? What evidence do they have?

Clifford has a hard job. His boss expects a lot from him, and he works in an unpleasant environment. "So, Clifford," I said, "when you get home dirty and tired, do you sit around and complain, or do you praise God for giving you a job and a family?"

After all, if Clifford just complains, why would anyone want to follow him? Who would want to be led where he's going?

Spending time with God
Exodus 33 describes how Moses would go to the meeting tent and talk with God face-to-face, like one friend talking to another.

But the part of the story we too often overlook is that of Moses's apprentice, Joshua. There the three of them would be in the tent, just Moses, Joshua … *and God.* Wow, how would you like to have been that kid? You'd get to listen in on conversations between God and Moses, one friend telling the other how the world worked and how he was supposed to lead the people. Okay, I don't know exactly what they talked about, but I do know that if God was talking, it was important.

If you could be Joshua in that tent, you would have the benefit of hearing God talk to Moses, and you would have Moses right there to help you understand what God was saying. You would get to hear and ask about Moses's plans to carry out what God intended. You would have an inside track on heaven and earth, how it all works, and what your next move should be. You would have the wisdom to lead nations … just as Joshua did.

Today every Christian has that same privilege. We can meet with someone even closer to God: his son. God instructs us to listen to what Jesus says (Luke 9:35). If we are his, we will know his voice and obey (John 10:27). God has promised never to leave us, and Jesus was clear about his mandate for us to be his witnesses. You can have the wisdom to lead your household … through obedience to God.

Be a man of integrity

A leader must be someone his followers can depend on—in other words, a leader who is trustworthy. Husbands too often forget this aspect of leadership. Ask yourself if you are someone who will make choices in favor of his family every time, no matter the circumstances. If you aren't sure, you likely have a problem with integrity.

Every time Clifford said, "I don't know," when asked about where he wanted to take his family, he revealed a lack of integrity. He could tell you that it was important for his kids to go to church and develop a relationship with Christ, but he could not say what he planned to do to help them do those things. He did not take the time to discover his family's direction on his own; he did not ask his wife for help; he did not pray for answers. So his "I don't know" was really "I won't help."

A man of integrity will spend time in prayer and consultation with his wife in order to better understand where he is to lead. He will read the Bible, fast, and pray—putting time and energy into getting himself ready to lead. He will make any sacrifice necessary to bring God's vision for his family to reality. He is more than a promise maker. He is a promise keeper.

Final leadership responsibility

According to Ephesians 5:35, a husband is to love his wife as Christ loves the church. This biblical directive scares a lot of men because they misinterpret it as needing to die physically for their wife ... right now.

Let's take a closer look at the way Christ loves the church. He came near to her with a plan for salvation and then walked it out with her. He prayed for her and with her, and he taught her how to pray when she didn't know how. He made the sacrifice of leaving his family and the family business behind for a life focused on nothing but his bride's welfare. Jesus knew what he was called to do because he listened to God the Father and did what God told him to do.

Your family needs a man of God to lead them to victory—the victory won when a godly man becomes the leader in his home and helps individual family members along the narrow path that leads to salvation. Show them that path as you walk it yourself.

Walking out leadership responsibility

Everything in us knows there is something bigger than us. We know there is something or someone that will have the answers we are looking for and provide the direction we need. We tend to look in all sorts of easy places first, but finally we realize we might have a problem with perspective. I'll illustrate my point with the stories of two guys who were lost and unable to see past themselves until, finally, Jesus came and helped them find a way to lead their households. One is that wee little man named Zacchaeus. The other is me.

Luke 19 is the story of Zacchaeus, who was so curious about this Jesus he had heard so much about that he climbed a little tree to see over the crowd. He knew there was something about Jesus that was important to his life; he just wasn't sure what it was. So he found a new spot where he could see: the top of a fig tree. Jesus spotted him there and immediately went to his house for dinner and fellowship. In return, Zacchaeus repented and proclaimed that the members of his household would from then on serve God in all they did. At that very moment, he and his whole house were restored to fellowship with God.

Just think: Zach was just too darn short to see over the crowd, so he ran ahead of the crowd and climbed a fig tree. It must have looked funny, this grown man perched in a spindly, short tree. Then Jesus put the spotlight on him ... I'll bet the crowd laughed at him.

Zacchaeus had been accused of cheating people his whole life, so when Jesus went to his house, everyone grumbled; they did not think Jesus should visit such a terrible sinner. But Zacchaeus was overjoyed and followed his words of gratitude with action: he promised to give half of all he owned to the poor and repay fourfold all those he had cheated. Now *that's* putting your money where your mouth is. At the end of the story, Jesus said, "Today salvation has come to the house." Zacchaeus had risen above the crowd to become a leader in his house. As a result, he led his whole household to the victory of salvation.

I was caught up in the hippie lifestyle of the seventies and was just too darn stubborn to leave it behind. Then a sign by the side of the road (no kidding) asked if I was fighting battles and promised answers to my questions if I would come inside a certain church and ask about them. A couple of months later, I went to that church with my wife to see if they had the answers I was looking for. I put on a three-piece suit because I thought that was how I had to dress, and we took a seat near the front because we thought that was the right place to be. We noticed right away that mine was the only tie in the room, and many people had on shorts. I must have looked funny, but no one laughed that I know of. Instead, Christ spoke to me and provided many of the answers I had been so desperately looking for.

For the next five weeks, the preacher taught specifically about something in my life I needed to leave behind. I'm not talking about giving up the smoking and drinking—those were minor compared to stuff like the hate and lust and jealousy and unwillingness to forgive. All those things had made me such a small man that I could not see God and lead my family, even on my best day. Thank God for Charles Woodbury and that little sign on Atlantic Boulevard. Today I am the leader of my home, and my whole household has victory.

Conclusion

A leader must be leading somewhere worth going. It is your responsibility as a husband to listen to God and go where he instructs you to go. Your wife and family need you to help them see the vision, and they will need your help as they try to follow it.

You are to love them as Christ loves the church. So listen to the Father's instructions, and act on them. Be ready to make the sacrifices necessary to lead your family in a life that leads to salvation and victory in Jesus.

Read ... Luke 19:1–10 and consider: is anything obstructing your view?

Pray ... Read Psalms 139:23–24 out loud. Ask God to help you discover anything that is keeping you from hearing him clearly.

Write ... You just prayed a bold prayer. Now take some time to write down what you hear from God about how you might hear him even more clearly.

Chapter 8

Lover

You are to **love** your wife as God loves you (1 Cor. 13:1–3). That is, you should **love** her unconditionally and like no one else can (Eph. 5:25). You are to prefer her over all things and at all times and in all of your actions (1 John 3:18); you should prefer her in all your words and thoughts (Mal. 2:15). Your wife will observe the fruit of the spirit in your life (Gal. 5:22–23). **Love** her exclusively (Prov. 5:15–19). Be the physical **lover** she needs (Song of Sol. 2:16; 1 Cor. 7:3–5).

Steve and Jennifer

Steve was an up-and-coming executive at a major insurance company. He shared a secretary, Billie, with two other executives in his department. Billie was a single mom with two wayward children; she always seemed to have problems that needed solving. She did good work for Steve, despite having to juggle kid troubles, an ex-husband who never helped out, and trying to keep her head above water on a secretary's salary.

Steve was a kind man, and he hated to see Billie struggle so much. So he helped her out from time to time by doing little fix-it jobs around her house and regularly picking up the kids from their various activities.

At first Steve's helpful acts didn't bother Jennifer; as a matter of fact, she was proud of her husband for being such a caring individual.

Then one weekend, Billie asked Steve to retrieve her son from a camping trip because her car wasn't working. Jennifer, meanwhile, wanted Steve to drive her to the beach. To Steve it was clear that this child needed a safe ride home more than Jennifer needed to go to the beach. So he went off on his act of mercy, failing to understand the disappointment he inflicted on his wife.

Jennifer wanted Billie to get her own husband and leave hers alone. She felt second to Billie and even wondered if Steve had feelings for her. *Will he leave me for her?* she asked herself. Their relationship was in trouble.

First and best ministry

A husband's first ministry is to his wife—period. If you ever feel like you are having to choose between ministering to your wife and to someone or something else, you are likely ignoring your wife. When you stood in front of witnesses at your wedding and said, "I do," you were saying, *I belong to someone, and she belongs to me.* She gets all your affection, help, advice, and everything else she needs. When you choose to share any of that with someone else, you need to have her permission *and* her blessing.

In this case, Jennifer was upset because someone else was getting some of Steve's best, and she wanted that for herself. That may sound selfish, and it is ... but it's right. This kind of jealousy is good. Jennifer was expressing a deep desire for all of Steve, not meanness toward Billie. This jealousy is the kind God meant when he told Moses, "I am a jealous God" (Exod. 20:3–6).

Husbands are called to love their wives—a mandate that can be found repeatedly in the Bible. Proverbs 5:15–19 tells us to love our wife exclusively and keep her for ourselves only, while the Song of Solomon is full of dedications to a man and woman who are desperately in love with one another. We promise to love and cherish in our wedding vows, and God himself deemed "very good" his companion creations of man and woman in the garden (Gen. 1:31). In 1 Corinthians, Paul tells us that without love we are nothing—no matter how generous, powerful, or otherwise wonderful we are.

Even if you know it is important to love your wife, you may be struggling with how to act out this critical aspect of marriage. I want to propose a novel idea: ask her. That's right—ask your wife things like, "How can I make your life better?" or maybe, "I love you and want to show you. Please tell me how." Be diligent in asking and then acting on what you hear.

Wives are taught by our culture that if they have to tell their husbands how to show their love, it won't be special. I know from experience that this simply is not true, and that by asking you can save yourself a lot of worry and heartache.

How do you say, "I love you"?

Early in our marriage I was constantly trying to show Gay I loved her. I would hear my friends brag about the expensive gifts they were purchasing for their wives, and I wished I could do the same for mine. At the time I had just graduated from college and was teaching sixth grade in an inner-city school. I was lucky to afford the gas required to commute to work in my 1972 Super Beetle; expensive gifts were out of the question. I was bummed.

On our second anniversary I took Gay to a midpriced chain restaurant for dinner. The best I could afford was the nightly special: dinner for two, plus dessert. Gay wore a simple dress she had purchased on sale. Again, it was the best I could afford. I remember sitting there, staring at the most beautiful woman I had ever known, and feeling guilty because I could not do more for her.

For fifteen years I would think about that evening and the guilt would return. I was embarrassed that I had not done better for her ... she deserved better. I wondered how she could love me and why she had stayed with me.

One night we were talking with another couple about our fondest memories and how they help us mark the love we have for one another. Gay told the story of our second anniversary dinner. She talked about how wonderful and exciting it was to have my full attention, how she had eaten strawberry crepes for the first time, and how delicious they were. "It was perfect and so much fun to just sit and enjoy time together," she said. Unlike my memories of that evening, Gay's memories reminded her of how much I love her.

The lesson? I wasted fifteen years feeling guilty because I did not have the courage to ask my wife what makes her happy. Turns out, she is more interested in spending quality time with me than in any gift I can buy her. Our honest discussion about it has offered me the opportunity to love her more fully.

The David Crowder band sings it like this: "He is jealous for me, loves like a hurricane." Nothing makes my wife happier than me loving her like the unstoppable force of a hurricane. Nothing is allowed to stand in the way of that love, nothing can quench my desire for her, and I am happy to pour out all I have for her if that is what she needs. I want to be guilty of telling and showing her I love her too much. I want her to be so drenched in the downpour, so windswept by the force of my feelings, that she has no doubt that I love her physically, emotionally, and spiritually.

Every husband should strive to know what his wife needs and make fulfilling that need his top priority, even above what he wants. So spend time listening to your wife—she will tell you what she needs—and then shower her with it. I am 100 percent sure that when you do, you will never be disappointed with the result ... I never have been.

Show the fruit of the spirit

"But the fruit of the spirit is love, joy, peace, forbearance, kindness, goodness, faithfulness, gentleness, and self-control" (Gal. 5:22–23).

Loving your wife "spiritually" is another important aspect of being the lover she needs. Let me suggest that we are called to be fruit inspectors. If the way we love produces joy, peace, forbearance, kindness, goodness, faithfulness, gentleness, and self-control, then it is likely of the Holy Spirit. If it does not produce those qualities, it certainly is not of the spirit. Too often we measure our actions by what we think is good. But if it does not produce fruit of the Holy Spirit, you should question how good it really is.

So what is "fruit"? Well, it is not the seed and it is not the plant. Rather, it is what is harvested from the plant after the seed has been planted and the plant has matured. Fruit is not only the food produced by the plant that nourishes us, but it is also the seed-bearing part of the plant. A single seed planted will produce many multiples of itself, ultimately feeding many more than would the single piece of fruit from which it came.

Remember that your having peace does not mean you have passed that peace along to your wife. For example, I think Steve was happy in his new role as Billie's benefactor. But Jennifer needed him, and for her, his actions produced the fruit of uneasiness, not peace. So while it was important that he love his wife, it was just as important that he love her in a way that produced the fruit of love in her.

The bottom line is this: when we display fruit, we are planting a seed. That seed, in turn, will grow into a plant that will produce fruit. So if I show my wife anger, I should not expect to produce a crop of kindness. If I am addicted to alcohol, cigarettes, or pornography,

I should not expect to produce a harvest of self-control. When I sow a seed of self-control, I reap a harvest of my wife's dedication to me. Sowing forbearance grows a harvest of her acceptance of and tolerance for my shortcomings.

Don't boldly go where you should not

James 4:1 spells it out: "What is causing all the quarrels among you? Isn't it your desires battling inside you?" Husbands need to end any quarrel by simply saying, "I will not go there … ever." Don't start down the path, and you will not end up where you should not be.

Things that distract you from giving your best love to your wife are often simple things presented in a seemingly innocent way.

I have a friend I have known since junior high school. We have supported each other throughout life's trials, successes, and failures. Like most friends, we talk regularly and very often about trivial things. For years, we would call one another on Sunday afternoons to compare the lingerie ads in the Sunday paper. He might call and say something like, "Did you see the J. C. Penney ad?" I would either agree that Penney's was the best or tell him why I liked another one. This seemed like innocent fun, but I know our wives must have been disappointed in the way we were enjoying pictures of other women in their bras and panties.

My friend and I have since stopped this habit and stopped the rough talk about women. In fact, I have stopped taking the Sunday paper and have asked my wife to help me by changing the channel when the Victoria's Secret models appear on TV. This may seem silly, but a big part of being dedicated to the woman I love and showing her good fruit in my life is to know my own limits.

Physical love

I want to go on record right now and say that our God is an awesome God. First he invented women, and I think that was a pretty good day's work. But he did not stop there: he then invented sex. Sex is physical love reserved for married couples. It is God's wedding gift to us, and it is important to a healthy marriage.

The evidence that sex is important to marriage is the massive effort Satan has put into perverting it. Pornography is the biggest business on the Internet, prostitution is legal in some areas, and it is common and often advised for couples to fornicate before they are married. What a mess. The worst product of this perversion, however, is the corruption of the definition of sex and what makes good sex.

Sex, adultery, and fornication

This is an area where the standard has been lowered and, in many cases, the surrender flag is up. Many couples have never been taught the difference between sex, adultery, and fornication, and so they have trouble with them. Let me clear that up right here:

- **Adultery** is when married people have physical relations with people to whom they are not married. The socially accepted term for adultery is *having an affair*. I am of the opinion that an affair is something you have in the backyard around the pool, with all your family and friends. What most people call an affair is actually something you would be embarrassed to invite the neighbors over for. God called adultery a sin in the Ten Commandments. You should, too.

- **Fornication** is when people have physical relations as if they were a married couple, but they are not married. The socially accepted phrase for this is *sleeping together*. (My wife thinks this is a curious reference because there isn't much sleeping going on.) I wonder if more parents would support bringing back the tradition of chaperones if someone started keeping statistics on teen *fornication* rather than teen sex. Again, God calls this act a sin in the Ten Commandments.

- **Sex** is when married people have a physical relationship. It is a wedding gift from God. He invented it and reserved it for the marriage bed. When we begin to call adultery and fornication by the same name, we dishonor this gift.

A study conducted by the National Center for Health Statistics[3] shows that as many as 70 percent of couples live together before they marry. Those same studies tell us that couples who cohabitate before marriage have nearly double the divorce rate of couples who do not. If you lived with your wife before you were married and you have not confessed this as sin and accepted Christ's forgiveness for it, there's a place for Satan to have a foothold in your marriage. So take just a moment right now and settle this issue. Pray with your wife, receive the forgiveness of Jesus, and erase this sin from your marriage—forever.

If you prayed for forgiveness for a past sin of adultery or fornication, write a note to yourself here and date it. Perhaps accompany that entry with a reference to John 8:10–11. If Satan ever tries to remind you of that past sin, show him this written proclamation. Never accept condemnation for that sin again.

Intimacy at its best

Praying together is the best intimacy you will ever have with your wife. It will lead you to know the desires of her heart—what's really important to her—so you can agree with her in prayer. She will hear your heart as you approach God together, as a one-flesh team.

Look at how Adam and Eve related to one another: "they were naked and unashamed." *Naked* means more than "without clothes"

---

3 From the National Center for Health Statistics, based on data from the Centers for Disease Control and Prevention's National Survey of Family Growth, March 2010.

here; it means there was no dishonesty in them and no sin between them. Adam hid nothing from Eve, and Eve shared everything with Adam. They knew each other and were honest with each other. They had intimacy—each inviting the other to "into-me-see."

Praying together may take practice, and that's okay. You may feel uncomfortable at first, and your prayers may feel forced or shallow. If you are in the habit of praying only silently and only by yourself, praying together may feel like a violation of privacy. If this describes you, take small steps at first. Take turns praying aloud before meals, reading the Bible to one another, or offering a quick prayer for safety before you leave for work in the morning. You will soon crave even more honesty and more open prayer time together. Before long, you will desire to have your wife, who is your perfect helper, praying with you.

Gay and I have counseled countless couples on the subject of intimacy. Many have told us that improving their prayer life together led to an improved sex life. One young couple reported to us that their prayer life was taking up more and more of their day, and we were impressed by their spirituality and dedication. The wife explained that the prayer was wonderful and they had never been more in love—but the irresistible and satisfying sex afterward was becoming very time-consuming. Remember, Adam and Eve were closest to one another when they walked together with God daily. "Naked and unashamed" is God's desire for every married couple.

Conclusion

Your responsibility as a lover has many facets: spiritual, physical, and intellectual. You are to love your wife more than you love any hobby, more than you love any other person on earth. Be sure she sees you act that way.

Be naked and unashamed with your wife. Invite her to be honest with you about what says "I love you" to her. Pray with her and sow seeds that produce the fruit of the spirit. These actions will increase your intimacy, spiritually and physically.

Read ... 1 John 3:18, in which God is calling us to love not with words and talk but with our actions. Then read Galatians 5:22–23, which lists the fruits of the spirit.

Pray ... for God to show you the fruit being produced by your actions. Pray for the courage to be open and honest with your wife when you ask her how to say, "I love you."

Write ... about the fruit you are seeing in your life, good and bad. Where did it come from?

If you prayed for forgiveness for a past sin of adultery or fornication, write a note to yourself here and date it. Perhaps accompany it with a reference to John 8:10–11. If Satan ever tries to remind you of that sin, show him this entry. Never accept condemnation for that sin again.

Chapter 9

• ◆ •

Standard Bearer

As a husband, you are to uphold the **standard of holiness** over your home (Exod. 17:15; John 14:23). You are to recognize God as the authority (Matt. 8:5–10). You are called to teach God's Word at all times (Deut. 6:6–9), teaching through your words and deeds (Luke 6:44–45). You are to serve your family and prepare them for a walk with Jesus (John 13:1–7).

A flag or banner is sometimes called a "standard." A company of soldiers going into battle may have more than one standard flying over their heads; it tells everyone who they are and for whom they are fighting. For example, you might see the American flag and know they are U.S. Soldiers, while flying right next to it is the standard for that particular group of soldiers, revealing something about the history of the unit and what they do. A company of soldiers will fight very hard—even to the death—to keep the standard held high for all to see. When new territory is won, the flag is raised over it to mark that claim.

It is the responsibility of the husband to raise the standard of holiness for his family and to keep it flying over them until they are ready to start their own families. You raise this standard by your own example. A successful man leads his family with a standard of holiness. He is not afraid to raise the banner of God in his home, and he chooses to follow God's precepts and commands.

Tim and Opal

Tim met Opal in church camp when they were sixteen. She lived in a nearby town in rural Illinois; they went to different high schools but belonged to the same Christian denomination. Because they both had been raised in the church and both sets of parents farmed, Tim and Opal had a lot in common. They courted all through high school and college and finally married after a long engagement.

Fast-forward nine years. They had moved away from the farm to follow Tim's career as a systems analyst, and God had blessed them with three children and a nice home. They were members of a local church of the same denomination in which they were raised. But to say they were "living the dream" would be an overstatement.

When they came to us for counseling, Opal told us it was hard to get Tim to go to church with her, and when he did, he complained about it. Tim, on the other hand, said he expected more from church than just a bunch of "How ya doing" and "Oh, I'm fine. You?" He said all the fake cheerfulness made him mad … the whole congregation was just a bunch of hypocrites. And yet both Opal and Tim said they wanted their children to have a relationship with the church. This one problem had become a source of many arguments and much ill will between them.

"Tim, do you believe the Bible is true?" I asked.

"Mostly," he replied, "but I think a lot of the Old Testament is outdated."

"Tim, do you think Jesus is Lord of Lords and King of Kings?"

"Of course I do."

"Is he lord of your life and king of your house?"

Tim thought for a long moment before he responded, "I am not sure."

Before you think badly of Tim, ask yourself, *Who is the king of my house?* Don't answer too quickly; let's be sure you understand the question. Take a moment to reread what I wrote about the third responsibility of a husband, to raise the standard of holiness.

Tim was not sure who was king of his life. This is dangerous territory, to say the least—potentially deadly. Jesus taught, "Whoever is not with me is against me, and whoever does not gather with me scatters." (Luke 11:23) There is no fence to sit on—it is black or white. We are either serving God or we are not. Imagine Tim's surprise as he read Jesus's words. He knew then that he needed to decide what authority was to rule his life and the life of his household.

As for my house, we will serve the Lord

The arguments Tim and Opal were having were not really about which church to attend or how well the preacher spoke or whether the people were all fakes. Opal simply needed her husband to make the same declaration Joshua made in Joshua 24:15: "As for me and my house, we will serve the Lord." Husbands must decide whom their house will serve.

As husbands, we are responsible for giving the household to God and managing God's will for the family. This is not a question of whether you take your kids to church; Tim attended church his whole life and wanted his children to have a relationship with the church. This is a question of whether you will have a relationship with the living God and give him the keys to the front door of your home.

Keeping the Word of God at all times

Robert and Ruth were already ten minutes late for our 2:00 p.m. appointment when the phone rang. It was Ruth, calling to say they knew they were late and were on their way. Knowing they would be in a tizzy when they arrived, we put the teapot on and waited.

"Sorry we are so late," Ruth said. "We drove as fast as we could!"

"Yeah," Robert added. "Traffic was moving kinda slow."

Gay assured them it was okay and offered to take their coats and fix a cup of tea for them. She returned in a few minutes with tea for us all, and we talked about our last session together and how they were doing. After reviewing the homework we had given them the last time we met, we were ready for this week's lesson.

I opened with a question: "Robert, Ruth, have you ever considered what the first sin ever was?"

Ruth was quick to reply. "Yes, I think it was that they ate from a tree they weren't supposed to."

"Good. Can you remember what the name of the tree was?"

"I think it was the tree of knowledge."

Robert jumped in with, "No—I think it was the tree of the knowledge of evil."

They were so close. The forbidden fruit came from the "tree of the knowledge of good and evil" (Gen. 2:9). In other words, the tree offered the ability to judge good from bad. It was what Satan claimed would make Adam and Eve like God (Gen. 3:5); and it is also what God told them would kill them (Gen. 2:17). This fundamental truth played out at the beginning of human history is important for any husband planning to lead his family with the standard of holiness. God was generous and gave us everything except what was bad for us. But we decided to go against him, taking the thing that would kill us.

"So, Robert, how fast did you go when you hurried over here today?" I asked.

"I never went faster than eighty. Why?"

"What was the speed limit?"

"Most of the way it is fifty-five," he said. "That's when I was going eighty. But I was just going with the flow of traffic. And besides, I didn't get a ticket, so it must have been okay."

Anyone who knows me personally is aware that drivers' general disregard for the speed limit is a pet peeve of mine. I believe Christians who speed are thumbing their nose at God. The Bible is very clear when it tells us to submit to the government God has placed over us (1 Pet. 2:13). Yet given what appears to be a clear directive from God, I find that few Christians agree and actually refrain from "going with the flow of traffic."

Husbands have a huge responsibility to lead by the choices they make. Our choices should be according to God's Word, not what we think might be right. We must never exchange our own judgment for what God says, because the penalty for that is way more costly than the fine for speeding. When Adam and Eve ignored God's Word in Genesis 3, it cost all mankind direct access to eternal life and personal fellowship with God.

Mild forms of deception

Robert was "going with the flow of the traffic." This is a great metaphor for Satan's way of getting you to lower the standard of holiness over your life. Satan rarely attacks head-on; he would rather deceive you into letting him win a little at a time. James 1:14–15 tells us that "each person is tempted when they are dragged away by their own evil desire and enticed. Then, after desire has conceived, it gives birth to sin; and sin, when it is full-grown, gives birth to death."

I cannot tell you how many times I have caught a thirteen-and-a-half-inch bass when the keeper limit was fourteen inches, and I knew I could get to the cleaning shack before the game warden inspected my catch. I had a choice to make. No one would know but me, right?

Is it less adulterous if the stripper you hired for a bachelor party only stripped to her bra and panties? After all, lots of the other guys there were regular churchgoers, too.

If I only cheat a little on my taxes, is that okay? After all, I'm a nobody to the IRS. It's the big corporate cheaters they are after.

I'm a little short this week, so I won't give my 10 percent tithe—but I can make it up later.

Divorce is okay if I'm really unhappy. God wants us to be happy, doesn't he?

Don't fall for the lies you hear from the popular media: each one of these seemingly small transgressions will lead to death, according to James 1:15. In Matthew 5:28, Jesus tells us that just looking at a woman with lust is adultery, and in Mark 12:17 he makes it clear that we are to pay our taxes. In Malachi 2:16, God tells us that he hates divorce, and later on, in Malachi 3:9–10, he says we're thieves if we do not tithe. So why does Satan tell us otherwise? Because he wants us to lower the standard of holiness and, to let him take our territory from us.

Raising the banner in my home

In the earlier years of our marriage, Gay and I often had people over to our house to play music, swim in the pool, and generally hang out and enjoy the afternoon. Many of our friends would bring along a cooler of beer or some other "adult beverage," and as the day progressed, some folks would get quite drunk and start telling bad jokes, flirting with people to whom they were not married, or even getting into arguments. For perhaps twenty years we tolerated this bad behavior because, after all, these were our friends, and they did not usually act like that.

Finally, though, I gathered the strength to say to my wife, "I think we should banish alcohol from our property." Gay was surprised and asked how we could manage that. After all, she had a pretty good collection of fine bourbons, and she wasn't sure some of our friends would come over anymore if we did not allow them to drink.

"Are we just going to toss out hundreds of dollars' worth of expensive, well-aged stock?" she asked. "And what about your wine collection—does it go, too?" Ouch, that hurt. Somehow wine didn't seem as bad as hard liquor. Surely I could keep a couple of bottles of my favorite stuff.

Please understand—we do not think alcohol is evil. It is just a way for evil to get a foothold into the home. So we had to make a choice. We could banish alcohol, make a boundary that could not be crossed, and be prepared to defend that boundary, or we would constantly have to fight the enemy in our home and judge the people we loved. When we put it that way, it was an easy choice. But make no mistake: protecting the border is not a job for wimps.

Conclusion

God is in charge. Whether or not you believe that fact is immaterial. He is. When God says, "Let it rain," it does. When he says, "Stop raining," it does. He created things like gravity and light, so it's no wonder we don't completely understand them. He has asked us to do certain things and not to do certain other things. We need to take him at his word on that.

Husbands need to decide to serve the Lord. By doing so, they are raising the standard of holiness over themselves and their whole household.

Husbands are then called to uphold that standard of holiness at home so they can be in the presence of God as an example for their families.

Read ... Deuteronomy 30:11–20. God is presenting a simple choice. You do not need to go on a quest to find it. If you choose to obey God's way, you will receive prosperity and long life.

Pray ... for a clear vision of God's standard of holiness for your household.

Write ... your decision. Make a written declaration in your journal that you and your household will choose life and follow the Lord. This will serve as a reminder to Satan that this is one house in which he is not welcome.

Chapter 10

Provider

As a husband, you are to **provide** for the physical needs, the spiritual guidance, and the safety of your wife and family (1 Tim. 5:8). You also should **provide** training (1 Tim. 4:16), encouragement, and prayer for your family (Deut. 6:6–9). Your words and deeds must **provide** an example of a life that reflects the Gospel message (Rom. 2:13–14).

Tim and Opal

Tim had a demanding corporate job. He was expected to work long hours, travel a lot, and be available if something went wrong at one of the corporate locations. They paid him a great salary, and as a result, he could afford to buy his wife and kids lots of great stuff. But the great salary also required a great deal of commitment to his job.

"We were on vacation, Tim," Opal said. She was mad at Tim for missing a special dinner with the kids at Disney World.

"Opal, you need to understand that my boss called and needed me to take care of a problem," Tim said. "My job is more important than dinner with some cartoon characters. And besides that, you were there with the kids—and I got there for dessert. So it all worked out, right?"

Opal gave a heavy sigh and crossed her arms. Tim and Opal were definitely not on the same page about what the family really needed.

Tim looked from his wife to me and then to Gay, looking angry, frustrated, and puzzled all at once. He threw up his hands and shouted, "I just don't know what they want from me!"

What do they want from me?

The answer to this question can be elusive for husbands. If you don't know what your family needs, you can't hunt it down, kill it, and bring it home. So where do you look to find the answer?

Tim is not unlike many American men: he works very hard to provide for his family. When they want a new flat-screen TV, he wants to buy it for them. If one of the children needs braces, he wants to be able to afford it. When it comes time to pay for his daughter's wedding, he wants to be able get the best dress, the best hall, and the best caterer money can buy. We borrow money to afford new cars and the latest gadgets; we move to the most expensive neighborhood the bank says we can afford. To accomplish this, we work at a job that pays the best—even if we hate it and it requires us to sacrifice time with our family along the way.

The problem with Tim and the many other husbands like him is that he never asked what his wife needed. He was guessing about being in the right place and doing the right things. His actions were based on what he thought might be right or perhaps what he had learned in school, on TV, or from his parents. He was trying his best to be a good provider; the problem was, he hadn't considered what is most important according to the source of truth: the Holy Bible.

Good provider

Men are taught to measure their success as providers by the job they hold and the things they can buy—or how much money they will leave behind for their wife and kids when they are gone. Perhaps we should judge a man according to whether he enrolled his kids in soccer even though he couldn't really afford it, or according to the quality and price of his family's cell phones or gaming system.

Wrong, wrong, and *wrong*!

Jesus sums it up in Matthew 33:31–33: "So do not worry, saying, 'What shall we eat?' or 'What shall we drink?' or 'What shall we wear?' For the pagans run after all these things, and your heavenly Father knows that you need them. But seek first his kingdom and his righteousness, and all these things will be given to you as well." Here are the measures of a good provider:

- He gives his family a vision of the kingdom through the living example of his life.
- He is blessed in his walk and able to supply the physical needs of his family.
- He furnishes his family's safety through his fervent prayers.
- He gives his family God-inspired spiritual guidance.

If you are thinking this is a tall order, you're right. It is. But be encouraged in this promise: "my God will meet all your needs according to the riches of his glory in Christ Jesus" (Phil. 4:19). Celebrate the fact that you have a God who cares and will supply your needs. Your job is to seek him *daily*.

Seek provision daily

Like so many men, Tim did not pray for God's provision daily. As a result, he did not have sufficient provisions for himself, much less enough to pour out to his wife and family. God will supply your needs, but it is your responsibility to go out and gather them up every day. Today's provisions will not solve tomorrow's needs. God taught this lesson to the Jews in the desert, and it still applies to our lives today.

God called his people out of slavery in Egypt and sent them into a desert. They carried what they could with them, but they did not have time to prepare enough provisions for the long journey. There were more than six hundred thousand men in the group, so the Nation of Israel numbered more than one million people. Can you imagine? Just one meal from KFC would have been five hundred thousand buckets of chicken and who knows how many quarts of mashed potatoes and slaw. And that is just lunch on day one; they were in the desert for forty years.

So where did all the food come from to feed that many people on the move for forty years?

Every night, manna fell from the sky—white stuff that covered the ground around the Jews like dew on the grass. They were instructed to gather just enough for today, because God would provide for them every day. Sometimes people would try to hoard it, just in case God forgot, but the manna would spoil and have worms in it by the next morning.

What is manna? The Jews only knew that it was food and that God had provided it. Because they were not sure what it was, they called it *manna*, which translates to "What is it?"

The lesson a provider needs to learn from this story is that God gives us fresh spiritual provisions every morning. We cannot stock up on prayer for our family, or wisdom or vision, or guidance from the Holy Spirit. We need to gather new manna every day. Yesterday's manna is old, has worms and is not fit to eat or feed to your wife and family.

Providing spiritual guidance

Do not hesitate to provide spiritual guidance to your wife and children. The best way to do this is to live a life exemplifying a walk with Christ. In Matthew 5:15, Jesus tells us to "let your light so shine that others will see it and glorify the Father in heaven."

Doing this requires courage. You will need courage to stand in the midst of men who may not agree with your beliefs, saying no to things that don't reflect the life you want to display. You will need courage to say no to your boss when you are asked to give more than your family can afford in terms of your time or attention. Your light will shine—you will provide an example to follow—but you have to choose what that example will look like. Jesus knew this. He was just telling us what kind of light he would like us to shine.

Clarence Budington Kelland once said of his father, "He didn't tell me how to live; he lived, and let me watch him do it." This is by far the best way to provide spiritual guidance. Choose to seek God's righteousness, and your whole household will receive it.

Providing safety

Contrary to popular belief, even the best deadbolt and alarm system will not create a suitably safe place for your wife. Safety is significantly deeper than that. Secure doors and good locks will help keep her physically safe and will help keep thieves from taking her stuff, but what good is that if there is no tomorrow? Does she know that God loves her and has prepared a home for her? Have you assured her that every day you are praying for her and for direction for the family? Have you shown her that you will never leave her?

Your wife wants to know your plans and dreams. She wants to know what you are praying about, and she wants to pray with you. A woman feels safe with a man who casts a vision for his family and leads them toward it. She will feel safe when your words and actions align. When your life displays the fruit of the spirit, you're revealing your love for her, and she will feel safe.

Providing training and encouragement

The best training and encouragement a man can provide for his wife and family is a life well-lived. Your love and obedience to God are worth more than any gadget you can buy, any vacation you can afford, or the best Ivy League education. Love your wife unconditionally, and your sons and daughters will be encouraged to love and be loved.

When my dad caught my brother and me with some pictures of topless women, he did not spank us—we were too old for that. He did not ground us or take away our allowance. Instead, he made it personal. Dad took me aside and told me that he would not tolerate this level of disrespect for his wife. He was not asking me to respect my mother; I had already broken that trust. Instead, he was demonstrating how a man protects the woman he loves, no matter who is the offender.

Dad both taught and encouraged me with this lesson. I understood that women were to be respected and that I would one day be responsible for a wife and should demand respect for her. I was encouraged because my father took the time to teach me this lesson one-on-one. And it proved more valuable to me than the best meat on the table or the biggest house in town.

The last time I saw my dad alive was at his house in Florida. He was severely disabled from a stroke and sitting in a wheelchair. I loved the old man and missed the younger man who had taught me to fish and encouraged me to be strong and get an education. I knew he had prayed for me to find Christ all those years I was out in the world, doing all those worldly things. I knelt next to his chair and said, "See ya later, Daddy-O." He told me, "See ya, son."

I knew I likely would never see my dad this side of heaven again. He knew it, too, and he was telling me that we would meet again in heaven because God had promised us that. I miss the old man and often wish I could talk with him, but I know my redeemer lives because Daddy-O said so. And he was serious when he told me he would see me later.

The eight-hundred-mile drive back to my house was a wonderful time of loving reflection on my dad, who had provided spiritual guidance even with his last good-bye to me. With all the confidence of a man about to meet Jesus any minute, he showed me that heaven is real and worth striving for.

Walking it out

It will be nearly impossible for you to walk out this spiritual example on your own, so God has provided resources to help. God gave his Word as instruction and the Holy Spirit as a constant guide. God made his Word flesh in Jesus, and in your wife he created your perfect helper. God has provided these powerful weapons because there is an enemy out there who would like nothing better than to hinder your ability to fulfill your responsibility as provider. If you cover your home with prayer, he will flee, leaving you, your wife, and your family in peace.

Tim began to pray with Opal regularly—almost every day, at first. Before long, they both desired the daily provisions that come from prayer, and now they rarely miss a day. Tim still travels quite a bit and is still paid very well by an employer that expects a great deal from him. But now he has a clear vision of what his family needs, and God gave him the courage to talk with his boss about his need to be the provider for his family. Not only has Tim's boss honored that need, but he has begun to institute an initiative to make sure all husbands at his company can take time off to provide for their families. I think these changes came as a result of Tim praying with Opal for God to clear the way.

Opal now feels safe and has a much stronger relationship with Jesus because she has seen mountains moved. And their children are getting the godly instruction they need, because Tim is gathering fresh manna from God every day.

Conclusion

A husband is called to provide many things for their wife and family. Their physical needs are important, but encouragement, safety, and spiritual guidance are even more important. Your wife will feel safe when she sees you live out the Gospel and produce the fruit of the spirit.

Being the provider is a daily responsibility. You will be challenged each day in new ways and by new situations. Remember to pray daily so Satan will leave your family alone; he'll have no choice but to leave. Encourage your wife always, and be sure to provide safety for your family through your walk with Jesus Christ.

Read ... Matthew 6:19–33, a wonderful teaching from Jesus about God's provision for us, and Philippians 4:19, God's promise to supply from his glory—not because of who we are or what we can accomplish.

Pray ... because where prayer is, Satan is not, and where prayer is not, Satan is. Provide the prayer cover your wife and family need. Pray as specifically as you can about and for them.

Write ... a list of the things your wife needs from you right now. What is God showing you about those things and how they will come into your life?

Chapter 11

Warrior

The **warrior** is not afraid of the enemy, but instead is riled up by him (Deut. 20:2–3). You will battle against the power of darkness in all matters concerning your wife and family (James 4:7; Jude 1:22–23). As the **warrior** husband, listen to your wife when she discerns imminent attack from the enemy (Gen. 2:18). You should always be dressed in the full armor of God, ready to protect your wife and repel the enemy (Eph. 6:11–17).

Jim and Sheila

Sheila was crying when we opened the door to let her and Jim in. You could tell by the way Jim was acting that she was upset by something he had done. Turns out they had had a fight in the car on their way to the see their marriage counselors. How ironic is that?

Gay hugged Sheila and asked, "What is it?"

"We were fighting about our daughter," she answered. "She wants to try out for cheerleading."

"Oh," Gay said. "That's a good thing … isn't it?"

"I'm not sure. He wants to see the uniform she will be wearing in public first."

It turns out that Jim had taken a firm stand with his daughters about showing their midriff in public. He would not let them wear two-piece bathing suits and had them either tuck in their shirt or wear an undershirt. He was quite firm about it.

Sheila, on the other hand, was neutral on the matter most of the time, but she wanted Jim to soften the rule if it meant the girls could not be cheerleaders.

War requires an enemy

We have but one enemy, and it is Satan. He is the author of lies, a thief who comes to kill, steal, and destroy (John 10:10). He is your enemy, and he is relentless in his attacks on you and your family.

I like the way the hero in the first *Terminator* movie describes the evil robot to Sarah Connor. When she suggests that they just run away from the robot and hide from it, Reese has the following response: "Listen. Understand. That Terminator is out there. It can't be reasoned with, it can't be bargained with … it doesn't feel pity or remorse or fear … and it absolutely will not stop. Ever! Until you are dead!"

What I am trying to say is that Satan is serious, he is out there, and he hates you and your family. Unlike the Terminator, Satan is real.

Satan may not attack you himself and in person. He may set up a person, thing, or situation to commit acts of aggression toward you. Often the enemy comes in the form an illness or a job-related challenge. He also can attack your family through friends or even other family members. One of his favorite lies is to tell you that your wife is the enemy. I encourage you to stay focused. Your spouse is not your enemy—Satan is!

What makes a warrior

The most impressive characteristic of Reese in *The Terminator* is his confidence: he never doubts he will succeed. He knows why he has been sent, and he has his heart set on that mission. Reese knows the enemy has strength, the ability to track him down, and no other purpose beyond his destruction. His enemy is relentless in its desire to destroy him. Yet Reese finds success in focusing on something bigger than himself. He never takes his eyes off the prize; he is committed to standing firm against the enemy.

A warrior must be comfortable with who he is and why he's fighting; his heart must be in the fight. He must have a weapon capable of destroying his enemy and know how to use it. He must be receptive to intelligence about the enemy and act on it.

God has provided every husband warrior with clear marching orders to take a stand against the enemy. He has given every husband a wife as a prayer partner to help detect every enemy attack. The weapons God provides are not of this world, but they have divine power to demolish the works of the enemy. The warrior has the full armor of God with which he can take a stand against the enemy and his schemes.

War requires authority

Jesus told his disciples, "All authority in heaven and on earth has been given to me. Therefore go and make disciples of all nations, baptizing them in the name of the Father and of the Son and of the Holy Spirit, and teaching them to obey everything I have commanded you. And surely I am with you always, to the very end of the age" (Matt. 28:18–20).

Jesus is the general of this army, so any battle in which you find yourself is his, not yours. This is why the "inventory" described in the first three chapters is so important. When Jesus asks, "Are you for me or against me?" we must be able to answer clearly that we are on his side. Notice how Jesus defeated the enemy time and time again. He never fought against the people but rather the spirit behind their bad deeds.

The full armor of God

As warriors we are called to be dressed in the full armor of God (Eph. 6:10–8). We've been led to believe that the full armor of God is something we pick up when we're about to pray in troubled times or preparing to intercede on behalf of others—sort of like a dress uniform we wear to church or when we are around spiritual people. But the scripture warns us to stay dressed in full armor so that when the enemy attacks, we will be able to stand against him.

You are to be dressed this way:

- The **helmet of salvation** is the knowledge of your salvation. The time to decide that you are a blood-bought child of God is now, not when the battle starts.
- The time to guard your heart with the **breastplate of righteousness** is now, as well. Pray for God to search your heart and help you rid yourself of any anger, selfishness, lust, lack of charity, or other sin. Put on the breastplate and guard your heart so that the enemy cannot accuse you and cause doubt during battle.
- Have the **belt of truth** around your waist at all times. Satan is the father of lies and will use them to attack you. Have nothing to do with this tactic in your life.
- Take the **sword of truth** out of the sheath and keep it in your hand at all times. Be ready to strike the enemy, not ready to *get* ready to strike the enemy. Sometimes a weapon that's drawn, ready to strike, will scare off an attacker. So read your Bible every day, not just when trouble is on the rise in your life.

- Use your **shield of trust** (faith) to stop the flaming arrows of the evil one. The world tells us constantly that God is not real or that he cannot help us in certain situations. If you allow those lies into your thought process, you will begin to doubt. Simply trust God—period.

- Put on the shoes that are the **readiness that comes from the Good News of peace**. These are my favorite part of God's armor. I expect God to bring only peace into my life. Therefore when the enemy tries to bring unrest, I remind him that he cannot win, and I remain in peace.

The Story of King Ahab and Jezebel

Many of us use the word *jezebel* to mean a really bad woman—a prostitute or a party girl. But let's be clear about what the Bible says here. Jezebel represented the worst kind of evil: abandoning the worship of God and following other gods. She made it a practice to pervert those around her and destroy those she could not influence. She also reproduced, leaving seventy heirs who had to be destroyed in order to clean up her mess completely. For those unfamiliar with the Bible story, here it is:

King Ahab, the king of Israel, married Jezebel—or as 1 Kings puts it, "He not only considered it trivial to commit the sins ... but he also married Jezebel." According to the Bible, Ahab did more evil than any king before him. He committed murder, blasphemed, and generally did abominable things (1 Kings 21:26).

Ahab set up a Baal temple and began to worship there. *So he changed churches,* you might be thinking. *So what?* Please understand what a "worship service" at that church might look in modern times: Farmer Sam wants a better crop this year, so he pays a "temple prostitute" to have sex with him while his wife waits in the car. Or Charles and Gale are planning a room addition, so they take their third child and toss him into the fire as a sacrifice to ensure the project will go well (1 Kings 16:34).

In the time of Ahab, doing evil had become common and therefore trivial. Maybe the people of Israel justified their actions by saying something like, "Well, just this once won't hurt," or, "It's my only vice; besides, it's not hurting anyone else." The worst part is that the king did nothing about it. He took no stand against evil, and his family suffered terribly as a result.

As the king of Israel, Ahab had the means to buy and sell anything he could possibly imagine. His army was feared by all the surrounding kingdoms because it was protected by God. If he decided something was to be a certain way, it was—period. And yet he chose to act against God's law in various ways:

- He married a woman who worshiped other gods as higher than Jehovah, then aided her in that worship. (The First Commandment is broken, and a battle is lost.)
- He built Asherah poles and temples to Baal. Along with the poles came the temple prostitutes, the sacrifice of children by fire, and the raising of Baal above God. (Commandments two through six are broken, and the enemy wins another battle.)
- He and his wife stole a vineyard from an innocent man—in other words, he was a thief, showed no respect for his parents, and coveted his neighbor's things. (Commandments seven through ten are broken, the enemy wins the war against Ahab and his family, and they all die.)

The record of his life reads thus: "Ahab son of Omri did more evil in the eyes of the Lord than any of those before him" (1 Kings 16:30). As for Jezebel? She was thrown off a balcony, and dogs ate her until she was unrecognizable. And their kids, all seventy of them, were killed in an effort to blot out Ahab's legacy.

The saddest part of the story is that at any time, Ahab could have said, "I have lost some ground here," and returned to God for help. He could have battled against the evil in the land and saved his whole family.

Calling all warriors

Men like to think they are powerful. Do you ever walk by the mirror, flex just a little, and say, "Not too bad"? (Come on … I know I can't be the only guy who does that.) We think we're so bad—you know, bad to the bone, perhaps even the baddest man in the whole darn town.

If so, let me ask you a few questions: Are you bad enough to say to that mountain, "Go throw yourself in the sea"—and believe it will happen? If you are, then you should be able to tell your friends you simply can't make it to the bachelor party if a stripper will be there. You should be able to tell your boss that you can come into work *after* church so you can attend services with your wife and children. Are you man enough to walk out of a movie, turn off the TV, ask for the radio station to be changed? Jesus said we can have a faith so large it will move mountains (Mark 11:23). Perhaps we should start with some of the mountains that stand in our way as men of God.

Men, this is a call to action for every one of you. You need to become the defender of your home from all forms of evil. This means setting certain boundaries that cannot be moved or crossed. *You* need to set the standard for "normal" for your home. Don't let the world or your parents or your friends set it for you. It's time to put on your big boy pants and kick some butt.

When Jezebel was thrown off the balcony and onto the street to her death, it was a couple of eunuchs who threw her down. They had been castrated when they were young, and many considered them not to be men any more. But on that day, they showed what a real man is and does. They rose up against evil, even though they knew it could be their last act on earth.

Do you have friends who talk badly about marriage? Do your teenagers participate in activities you do not approve of? Do your parents, in-laws, friends, coworkers, or others pressure you and your wife into situations that don't line up with being a Christian leader? Here's an idea: be a mighty warrior, and stop it.

What happened to Jim and Sheila

Jim led his family in prayer to discern the right thing to do. Sheila agreed with her husband's vision for modesty for their daughters and told him so. She also felt a strong urging from God that other children could benefit from Jim's conviction (1 John 4:1–4). Jim spent time with his daughters to let them know that he loved them and had their best interest in mind.

Sheila also encouraged Jim to talk with the cheerleading coach about what he felt was appropriate dress for teenage girls. To his surprise, the coach agreed with him. Then Jim and Sheila helped that coach choose proper attire for young ladies to wear in public.

Over the course of this battle, Jim was careful to target the real enemy, Satan. His daughters were not the enemy. His spouse was not the enemy. The school system and even the coach were not the enemy. Satan was. Jim defeated the enemy with the humility of a son of God, dressed in the full armor of God.

Conclusion

We are at war, and as a husband you are called to be the champion warrior for your wife and family. Your wife is not your enemy, Satan is. You and your wife must pray to understand where the enemy wants to attack, and you are to take immediate and decisive action against it.

Because evil is present in the world, the warrior husband should always be dressed in the full armor of God and ready for battle.

Read ... James 4:7.

Pray ... for God to show you where the enemy is attacking your family right now. Is there sickness? Is there damage in a relationship? Ask your wife to pray with you. Talk about what God is telling you, and then move decisively against the enemy. He will flee.

Write ... what God is telling you right now about the attack of the enemy. Put Satan on notice that you will stand with your wife against him as a one-flesh team. Write down any scriptures that come to mind.

Chapter 12

Advocate

The **advocate** husband is always for his wife and against those who are against her, no matter the circumstances (1 Pet. 3:7). Therefore you will acknowledge her as the perfect gift from God (Gen. 2:18, 23). You are to represent your wife to Father God and at the city gates as without spot or wrinkle (Eph. 5:27).

The war department

Do you belong to a He-Man Woman Haters Club? Is there a group of guys with whom you get together to complain about "the old ball and chain?" This dynamic is so pervasive that there is a common language and set of signals used by the members of the club. One such term is *war department*, used to refer to a wife who may or may not allow her husband to have any fun and who might become angry when he asks.

Gay and I had been married for seven years and were living in Florida when my little sister, her new husband, and another couple who were mutual friends came to visit for the weekend. The six of us spent all day Saturday laughing and having a great time in the backyard. On Sunday morning we went to church and then on to lunch at a local barbecue place. Our visitors lived a couple of hours away and planned to leave for home later that afternoon.

The three guys were at the salad bar when someone suggested that we squeeze in a round of golf before they all had to leave. I said, "Well, I'm game, but let me check with the war department." My new brother-in-law headed back to the table before me and asked permission to play golf that afternoon. He also mentioned that Chris would like to go but had to clear it with "the war department."

When I returned to the table, my salad plate was not the only thing that was cold. Gay looked at me and then kind of wagged her head back and forth as she said, "The war department?" I just sat down quietly and ate my lunch. I would get to play golf later, but I also needed to apologize to Gay when I got home. I had hurt her; I had hurt her badly.

The problem here was that I was not being my wife's best advocate. I had talked about her in a mean-spirited way when she was not around. She must have wondered how I really felt about her. She was right: I did not see her in the right light. I wanted to be married to her and loved her dearly, but my words did not reflect that. My actions did not build her up; they tore her down.

What is an advocate?

An advocate is one who speaks positively on another's behalf. A good example of an advocate is the role a lawyer plays in the American criminal justice system. When you hire a lawyer, he will speak positively on your behalf no matter the circumstances. You may or may not be guilty, but as your advocate, your lawyer will claim you are innocent, and he will use every argument he can think of to prove you are not guilty. If the jury finds you guilty, he will appeal to another court for another chance to speak well of you. Your lawyer will never judge you; that's up to the judge and jury. His only responsibility is to tell everyone about your innocence.

It is a husband's responsibility to be an advocate for his wife. You are to speak of her beauty, her talent, her sweetness, and how she is your perfect helper sent from God. You are to brag about the wonderful love she has for you and how she cares for you. I personally take great pleasure when people tell me I am spoiled by my wife (and by the way, I am). And if I find someone who is not aware of how great Gay is and the fact that she spoils me, I am always ready to tell him.

Advocates don't judge

Your advocacy of your wife must not depend upon her performance. Your judgment about whether or not she deserves to be spoken well of at any particular moment has little to do with your responsibility as a husband and advocate. I am sure you will be disappointed in her actions from time to time, but this does not change your role as her advocate. Ephesians 5:25 tells us that a husband must be to his wife like Christ is to the church. I am so thankful that Christ's advocacy for me to the Father is not based on my performance. Our advocacy for our wives must be the same: constant and unconditional.

How to be an advocate

Proverbs 31 was written by a mother telling her son how to find a good wife, a woman of noble character. This good woman does many things for the family, the proverb says, and her husband is honored at the city gates because of her. I'll bet when he sits at the city gates and all the other guys are talking about the old ball and chain, he corrects them. He brags about his wife, telling them that she is a perfect gift from God. He admits he didn't deserve such a blessing, but God sent her anyway. Then he stops to pray that God will bless her wherever she is, right now.

There are several steps you can take to start being an advocate for your wife:

- Speak kindly about her to yourself, and remind yourself how much you love and cherish her.
- Speak kindly to her, compliment her, and tell her she is appreciated.
- Tell others that you love her. Don't hide it; brag about her. I enjoy telling my friends that they will have to settle for the second-best wife ever, because I married the best one.
- Pray for her. Tell God how much you appreciate the gift he gave you.

Men, consider these questions: What comes first, a woman acting on her ability to be profitable and of noble character, or a husband who believes in that ability and brags about her? I wonder what will come first, Christ bragging to the Father about me, or me being worth bragging about? How do you talk about your wife? Do you talk about her the same way, no matter who is listening?

Steve and Jennifer

"So, Steve—tell me what you see when you look at your wife," I said.

"She is very pretty," Steve said. "But she's also so darn stubborn sometimes that it drives me crazy." He then added, "It's like she wants to piss me off by being opposite girl or something."

"Is that all?"

"No. I see a woman that sides with her kids over me. And she never has been able to keep a budget. And she gossips with her girlfriends all the time—I think they just get together to complain about their husbands."

Steve was starting to get a little agitated, so I interrupted him. "Hold on, there. I think that's enough for now. Is that the woman you want to be married to?"

"Not at all," Steve confessed. "As a matter of fact, I didn't think that was the woman I married."

Jesus is our model for being a husband, and he is our model for being an advocate for our wife. The apostle John reminds us of how Jesus reacts to our shortcomings and sinful actions: "But if anybody does sin, we have an advocate with the Father—Jesus Christ" (1 John 2:1). We are to speak blessings about our wife to God the Father. We are to speak kindly to her and about her. We are to pray for her and thank God for the beautiful creature she is.

I asked Steve to begin praying for his wife and to be her advocate before the Father. He did, and their relationship began to blossom again. He set judgment aside and became thankful for her. The next time I asked him what he saw when he looked at his wife, he had a completely different answer—and he smiled when he spoke it.

Conclusion

Your wife is worth bragging about. She was created as the answer for your loneliness and your need for a "helper suitable." She is a gift from God himself, who created marriage to allow you to enjoy the fullness of her.

Your wife needs you to love and cherish her. She needs to know you love her and will stand up for her, no matter what.

Read ... Ephesians 5:25–27. You are to be proud of your wife and ready to present her without spot or wrinkle, just as Jesus is proud of you and presents you favorably to the Father.

Pray ... Take time right now to thank God and to thank your wife. Present her to God as that perfect helper, without spot or wrinkle.

Write ... about this subject, and take your time. Perhaps list some of the things you love about your wife. Be honest. Whether it is the shape of her nose, the way she makes gravy, or even the way she looks in blue jeans, write it down.

Chapter 13

Intercessor

You should be in constant prayer, thanking God for your wife and **interceding** for her benefit—and praying *for* her, not *about* her (Luke 22:31–32). Pray in the spirit, vigilantly and persistently for her (Eph. 6:18).

Intercession for your wife

To *intercede* means to come between and be in favor of. Too often, when we pray for someone we become tattletales, simply listing all that person's troubles. This is not intercession; it requires no faith at all. You are just reporting on a situation, hoping that maybe something will happen. Faith speaks about a person or situation the way God sees it, not how it is. Here's an example:

Gay and I had been married for sixteen years when she was diagnosed with a "large mass" in her abdomen. The doctors were pretty sure what it was and immediately referred us to an oncologist—a cancer specialist. You can imagine what a shock this was to Gay; it was as if the doctors had given her a death sentence.

Before we went to see the oncologist, I began to intercede. I prayed that this would be something else and that there would be a non-life-altering method to cure it. Gay prayed with me, and together we created a vision for her life that did not include cancer.

The mass still had to be removed and biopsied, but even before the surgery we knew it was benign. We knew because we had prayed for God to show us his vision for this situation. He did not show us a vision of Gay being healed of cancer, but rather a vision of her not needing cancer treatment at all.

Have you prayed for your wife today—not about her, but *for* her? Praying *about* her is telling God you need her to change or perhaps that you are tired of her acting like a witch. Praying *for* her is being her advocate and asking God to show you his vision of her.

Intercession, not judgment

Jesus hung on a cross and died for each of us. As he hung there, he was made fun of, spat upon, poked and beaten, and finally stabbed in the side with a spear. But with his last breath he interceded for us when he said, "Father, forgive them." He did not judge us—he interceded.

He rose from the grave and has ascended to heaven where he sits at the right hand of God the Father almighty. From this position he does not judge us, but instead intercedes for us. I like to imagine that he is telling God right now that I am perfect and holy enough to come home one day. I hope he's saying how beautiful I am and that I look just like him because I am one of his blood brothers. That's intercession!

I believe that if you are judging an individual or his circumstances, you cannot intercede for him. How often do we hear a prayer request from someone and right away get busy thinking about how to fix his problem? We are judging him when we pray that way. We need to be careful that we're not just trying to turn his situation into something *we* are comfortable with; this kind of prayer always keeps us from hearing what God has to say about the matter. True intercession means coming before God on behalf of another and asking him to help. Period.

Prayers that judge sound something like this: "If only Aaron would get a job, I am sure his life would be better. Lord, help him get a job." Or perhaps, "Father, I know Susan would be healthier if only she would stop smoking. Lord, help her stop smoking." Maybe Aaron does refuse to look for a job or Susan is defiant about her smoking. But changing their hearts is the job of the Holy Spirit, and you cannot be the Holy Spirit for anyone … not even your wife. An intercessor prays for the individual to receive a blessing, believes that God has a plan, and prays for that plan to come into existence. An intercessor does not try to change the person for whom he is praying.

Intercession takes a thankful heart

Jesus said that where your treasure is, there your heart will be also (Luke 12:34). If you have been given a treasure, you usually are thankful to the giver for that treasure. I ask you, have you thanked God for the miracle of your wife today? If not, I encourage you to stop right now and simply say thank you. You will feel your love for her grow, immediately and miraculously.

One of the most important exercises Gay and I have couples complete during counseling is a written faith vision for one another. This is difficult because it requires them to see their spouse as God does, even before he or she shows any progress toward being that person. A faith vision is, however, very beneficial to a marriage, because it helps you understand how to pray for your spouse. You'll recognize how God sees your wife, and you can begin to love her as God does by asking for his guidance as you begin to write for a faith vision for her.

Faith vision for your wife

When God created Eve, he created the perfect helper for Adam. She was the answer to what was missing in his life. Adam was not absent during the process; God presented all of creation to him and "no helper suitable" was found for him (Gen. 2:19). This tells me that Adam had some idea of what he needed and told God about it. He had a vision of what his wife would look like, and he knew he could depend on God to create her.

When I was younger, I thought I was a man of faith because I attended church and read my Bible—yet I could so easily call my wife "the war department." My problem was that I was walking by sight, not by faith. If the last thing I saw my wife do was resist my desire to play golf, then she was the war department. If the last thing I saw her do was make love with me, she was the greatest wife ever. I based my thinking on what I could see—not on God's vision of the perfect helper he had created for me.

Ask God to show you your wife through his eyes. I promise that the sight will be beautiful and wonderful. Your wife is the apple of his eye and the answer to his observation that "it is not good for man to be alone" (Gen. 2:18).

Satan would like to convince you that your wife is not the woman for you. I know from experience that when you are angry with your wife for any reason, it is easy to let your thoughts move that direction. A faith vision provides an anchor to hold onto and an objective for your prayers during stormy times. It is easy to defeat the enemy with your clear vision when his only weapons are lies and deceit.

How to write a faith vision for your wife

Hebrews 11:1 says that faith is confidence in what we hope for and assurance about what we do not see. So start by searching your heart to make sure you are walking by faith and not by sight. An example of walking by sight is tithing only when you have money to spare;

it takes real faith to give 10 percent when you are worried about whether the remaining 90 percent will feed your family.

Here are the next steps in creating a faith vision:

- Spend some time in prayer asking God to show you your wife through his eyes. When you pray for her, brag to God about her. He will brag along with you, and you will hear wonderful things you may not have thought about before. Remember, God loves her more than you do and has placed her in your life as a perfect helper.
- Take some time to search the scriptures for blessings for her. I personally like the Books of Wisdom (Psalms and Proverbs).
- I have spent hours watching and listening to my wife and hearing from God about who he says she is. I like to write those observations in my journal.
- Pray for wisdom, dreams, and visions about your wife (Joel 2:28).
- Finally, write down your faith vision.

A faith vision will never curse but will always bless. As you write your faith vision for your wife, be careful to avoid the common pitfall of writing a list of all the things you would change about her, or all the scripture she is failing to fulfill. The intent is to provide a prayer focus of thanksgiving.

Sharing your faith vision with your wife
One day, while Jesus and his disciples were walking along, he asked, "Who are people saying I am?" They offered a variety of answers, but he followed up with, "But who do you say I am?" When Peter confessed Jesus to be the Christ, Jesus told him that "no man has revealed this to you, no, it was my Father in Heaven" (Matt. 16:17).

Please share your vision with your wife. Nothing will tell your wife you cherish her more than knowing you are praying the will of God for her life. When you share, ask for her feedback—there may be things in her life for which she wants your prayer support. If there are, search the scriptures together and add this intention to your vision of her. Then invite her to create a faith vision of you that she can use to pray for you.

Walking it out

Steve decided to believe God's vision of his wife and walk it out. When Jennifer had a bad day, Steve interceded, commanding Satan to leave her alone. When she was happy, he thanked God for blessing her. As Steve sought a faith vision for Jennifer, prayed for it to come to pass, and kept his judgment out of the way, he fell deeply and hopelessly in love with his perfect helper.

At some point he shared his faith vision with Jennifer, and she responded by telling him how proud she was of him. She had never in her life experienced the kind of love and care Steve was showing her. That he would take the time to listen to God and search the scriptures on her behalf was more than she had ever expected of him. Steve's prayers for Jennifer are answered on a daily basis, and their relationship with one another and with Christ has steadily grown.

Conclusion

A husband needs to love his wife enough to know what God has to say about her. Once he knows God's plan, he needs to have faith that God will bring it into existence. Writing a faith vision for your wife will help you provide focused intercession on her behalf.

True intercession involves no judgment. God created every woman as an answer to the needs of a man, and he has a plan to make every married couple prosper. Husbands are not called to make their wives "straighten up"; they are called to pray for the manifestation of God's plan for their wives. Husbands should pray with a grateful heart, thanking God for creating the perfect helper and allowing him to enjoy her.

Read ... Matthew 16:13–19.

Pray ... for God to allow you to see your wife the way he sees her.

Write ... your faith vision for your wife. Who do you say she is?

Chapter 14

Forgiver

E very husband is to be an instrument of God's **forgiveness** (Exod. 34:9). Therefore you must **forgive** always and in all things. You should be the first to reassure your wife that you love her (1 Pet. 4:8) and have **forgiven** her (Matt. 6:14–15); do so even before she offends (Rom. 5:8).

God's plan for forgiveness

I was sitting at my mom's house one evening, just visiting with her—it must have been near the Easter season—when she began to tell me the story of Jesus's death from a mother's point of view. You see, like Mary, Mom watched her son suffer and die, and she could do nothing to stop his pain and eventual death.

My little brother died when he was just thirty-four years old. He was divorced and lived near enough to Mom that they had coffee together every day. Then he developed lung cancer, and she began taking care of him. He hurt a lot for eight months, and then he stopped hurting on December 26—just hours after we had had communion together in his hospital room.

Mom understands how it feels to watch helplessly as your son suffers. She was there when her son took his last breath, and she could do nothing to give him one more. She knows the anguish Mary felt watching her little boy being dragged through the streets. She knows the sorrow of calling out to God, begging him to let her son come home with her again.

As Mom spoke, she and I both were crying, remembering Clay and missing him. Then she did something she rarely does: she changed gears abruptly to teach me something about the nature of God. She said, "You know, Chris, I'm sure Mary was there when Jesus died, and there was nothing she could do. God, on the other hand, could have done something about it—and did not. He must really love us to have been able to watch the pain, suffering, and death of his only son just to provide forgiveness and a restored fellowship for us."

I have never lost a child to death. I do not know what that feels like. I do have a son whom I love so much that when he stubs his toe, it makes me want to cry. But God loved the world so much that he walked through all that pain and loss to provide forgiveness and restored fellowship for us all. My mom knows personally how painful it is to watch your child die; she's told me that she is not sure she could love the world that much.

Our response to being forgiven

Does forgiveness sometimes require sacrifice? You bet it does; God had to give his only begotten son so that you and I could be forgiven. Does it have its rewards? You bet; Jesus said that we will be forgiven in the same way we forgive. (Remember how he taught us to pray? "Forgive us our debts as we also have forgiven our debtors.") There is no loophole that will justify our failure to forgive. You can either forgive all things and be forgiven for all things or … not (Matt. 6:14–15).

Our response as Christians to the gift of God's forgiveness should be complete abandonment of self so we become one who forgives. As husbands we must lead our families by being one who forgives always—quickly and completely. We are to be so constant in our forgiveness that our wives know there is no offense we will not pardon completely. We are to be so quick in our forgiveness that our wives know we have forgiven them even before a trespass happens. We are to be so complete in our forgiveness that they know no forgiven offense will ever be held against them.

How to forgive

I am a man, so I will read the owner's manual only if I absolutely have to … and only after I have tried to do whatever it is myself and failed a bunch of times. But sometimes I'll also try something I've seen work for another guy … again, only after I have tried on my own first. Well, I have tried and failed to forgive so many times that I finally developed a step-by-step "forgiveness guide" to follow. Here is what works for me:

1) Concentrate on yourself. Remember that you are doing the forgiving; this process has nothing to do with what someone else may or may not do.

2) Ask God to show you his vision of the offender. God sees even the vilest offender as someone worth sending his son to die for.

3) Choose to forgive as an act of loving obedience to God.

4) Take the offense to the cross and exchange it for the love of Christ Jesus.

5) Confess it as done.

6) Remember the offense no more—instead, replace it with scripture (Mic. 7:19).

I've used these simple steps successfully over and over with couples from all walks of life and in all stages of their relationship. If there are instances in your life when you have failed to forgive, try this simple approach.

How often do I have to forgive?

I think Simon Peter must have been a great big guy. No doubt it helped his ego when Jesus chose to walk with him and then started calling him "Rock." Just think—wherever they traveled, Peter could introduce himself by saying, "Hi, my name is Simon, son of John. But the son of God calls me Rock." I always wanted a cool nickname like that.

I believe that Jesus was a fairly big guy, as well. I mean, he spent the first thirty years of his life as a carpenter. Back then things weren't just made of wood; often they were made of stone, or some combination of those materials. Lifting that heavy wood and stone and working with hand tools would have made Jesus a rugged individual in his own right.

One day Peter asked Jesus, "How many times must I forgive?" I wonder if Peter was fed up with someone and looking for a way to break off the relationship. He wanted to know the official rule, the standard number of times he had to forgive … like, was seven enough? As a Jew, Peter was used to going to the temple and asking a rabbi what the law said about his rights in a particular matter. So in his question to Jesus, he was simply asking his rabbi for a ruling.

I can imagine Jesus putting both his hands on Peter's shoulders, looking him in the eye, and saying, "How about seventy times seventy—how will that work for ya, big guy?" Peter likely took a step back and did some quick math … *What, 490 times? Man, I'll never be able to stop forgiving and walk away from this guy.* But before Peter could protest what likely seemed to him an unfair ruling, Jesus told a parable about forgiveness. Its conclusion? "This is how the Father will treat you, unless you each forgive your brother from your hearts" (Matt. 18:35).

How often must we forgive? To quote Buzz Lightyear: "To infinity and beyond."

Important note: If the repeated opportunity to forgive comes as a result of a destructive pattern in a person's life, you need to help that person with the cause of the problem. For example, if your brother-in-law is constantly wrecking your car because he drinks and drives, you should help him get help for his alcohol problem. If your wife constantly curses or is physically abusive, you should help her get counseling.

The atmosphere of forgiveness

When you practice forgiveness, you become known as "one who forgives." When you become a person known to forgive, you are creating an atmosphere of forgiveness in your home. But just like any new skill, learning forgiveness takes understanding and lots of practice.

Men have a strong desire to play to win. To win any game, you must know the rules, the layout of the field, and how to score. Men will work very hard on a very small aspect of any game if it will help them build an overall winning strategy. In order to win, a man will stand in front of a basketball goal for hours and miss shots all day long to learn how to make one.

At the same time, every man's toy box has something in it that was supposed to turn him magically from mere competitor to champion. I personally have owned ankle weights that were supposed to make me run faster, a trick golf club that was supposed to make me hit the ball straighter, and a "power tab generator" that was supposed to make me play guitar like Jimi Hendrix. I never did run fast enough to play baseball, I have long since given up golf, and don't look for me to be invited on stage to stand in for Eric Clapton. Conclusion: none of these gimmicks could replace good old practice.

We need to practice forgiveness so that it becomes our natural and automatic response to offense. I call this process "building an atmosphere of forgiveness in your home." Often the problems in a marriage come not because we don't try, but because we haven't taken the time to develop a shared vision. I think there are more misunderstandings in a marriage than there are disagreements. So help your wife be a better wife. Don't push her away with anger and accusations about her behavior.

Conclusion

A husband is called to be the model of forgiveness for his wife and family. You are to forgive as often as it takes to mend relationships—restoring fellowship first with your wife, and then with others. You are to establish an atmosphere of forgiveness in your home. Being ready to forgive even before there is an offense is the way of the Gospel. Your example will bring your family into closer fellowship with one another and with God.

Forgiveness is an act of will, not a feeling.

If there are repeated offenses, forgive every one of them—but pray to understand your role in helping the offender with destructive life patterns.

Read ... Matthew 18:21–35, in which Jesus instructs us about forgiveness.

Pray ... for peace and strength as you set an example for your family and forgive time and time again.

Write ... a list of any areas in your life where you need the victory of forgiveness. This will put Satan on notice that he will not have victory in your relationship.

Chapter 15

Reconciler

E very husband is to be an instrument of God's **reconciliation** (2 Cor. 5:18–19). You should stand ready to do the work of **reconciliation** (Isa. 6:1–8), modeling it through your actions, and only when necessary through your words (Col. 3:12–13).

Jim and Sheila

"Well, she let me down again," was what I heard as soon as I picked up the phone.

Sheila had made a habit of making promises to Jim and then letting other "important" things get in the way. There was the time she had agreed to go with him to a boat show in a neighboring town. The boat show was something Jim looked forward to all year, especially if he got to take his favorite girl, Sheila. So he bought the tickets, made arrangements for the kids, and even made reservations for dinner at one of Sheila's favorite restaurants for after the show. He wanted to make sure the whole day would not be just about him. Just two days before the big day, Sheila promised to help a friend move and canceled with Jim. She explained that her friend was going through a tough time and needed her support.

I had seen this situation before, and I knew Jim was really hurt. It did not matter what the letdown was—what mattered was the fact that his *wife* had let him down. That tore at him in a way nothing else could. "Why does she treat me this way?" he would ask—a request more for sympathy than for an answer. I would just sit quietly and let him talk. "I know Sheila loves me," he'd say, "and I know that this is not the end of our relationship."

Still, this was a real setback in their ability to fellowship. He was hurt, and she must be, too—why else would she treat him this way? But where was she hurting? And how could Jim help her with that? He did not want to be her therapist; he wanted to be her husband.

"She just needs to suck it up and stop being so selfish!" he shouted into the phone.

I came back at Jim firmly. "Okay, I hear that it hurts, and I know you don't want to continue this way. Have you told Sheila?"

"Well, not exactly," he said. "She knows I'm unhappy about it, though."

"Hmm … are you *sure* she understands what you need from her?"

In marriage we are called to renounce self and become as one flesh with our spouse. Husbands must love their wives unconditionally, forever—even when they are acting unlovely. Jim needed to forgive his wife before she came home from wherever she was. Then, from that place of forgiveness, he needed to be honest with her and make sure she knew what he needed.

Their relationship was not broken; however, their ability to have fellowship with one another was in real trouble.

Reconciliation

Reconciliation is the restoration of fellowship in a relationship. A husband's responsibility is to be a reconciler within his family; he is to help his wife and family forgive one another, even when it's hard to do.

When a couple is married, they start the covenant relationship that God says should never be broken. If you are married, you know that two becoming one can cause some friction—and when that happens it becomes hard to fellowship together. Or as Gay says to me when I've caused the friction, "I love you. I just don't like you very much right now."

Reconciliation is God's will for us. God instructed Noah to build an ark and then placed a rainbow in the sky as a sign of his promise to restore fellowship to man. Moses was sent to take God's people out of Egypt to a place where they could fellowship with him in freedom. Jeremiah, Isaiah, Ezekiel, and the other prophets were sent to tell God's people that he loved them and wanted fellowship with them. Finally, God sent his son to be our source of forgiveness so that fellowship could be restored.

Forgiveness and reconciliation

Where there is no forgiveness there is no fellowship—no huggy, no kissy, no warm smile from your lover, none of those things that make married life wonderful. If you go to bed mad at your wife, I hope you sleep well … but you won't. There will be a cold spot next to you where there is normally a warm spoon and a goodnight kiss. Or in the words of the Righteous Brothers, "You've lost that lovin' feeling."

To forgive is a choice. Let me clear about that: you choose to forgive or not to forgive. We forgive when we relinquish our right to be mad, hurt, or disappointed in someone and exercise our responsibility to be an example of God's loving kindness. It is pure and simple selfishness when we decide our wife has done something so ugly that we choose not to forgive her. We are raising our right to hold the hurt of that act in our heart above our responsibility to forgive.

This kind of selfishness is a real marriage killer. When we see a husband and wife who nurse grudges against one another, you can bet there is very little fellowship going on. When Adam and Eve sinned and broke fellowship with God, he could have just said the word and they would have been no more; he could have started all over again. But that is not the way of God. Instead, he sent his only son to die and provide forgiveness for our sins so that we could be reconciled to the Father and have perfect fellowship again.

If you have not forgiven, you have broken fellowship as well. This is such a big deal that Jesus said, "Therefore, if you are offering your gift at the altar and there remember that your brother has something against you, leave your gift there in front of the altar. First go and be reconciled to your brother; then come and offer your gift" (Matt. 5:23–24). In other words, he was telling us that if we have broken fellowship with our wife (or others), we have broken fellowship with God, as well.

When you forgive, you open the door for reconciliation. If you do not forgive, there can be no reconciliation. Both these words—*forgive* and *reconcile*—are action words; they are things you do. Forgiveness will not happen on its own. You must do it.

How to reconcile

The next time you feel angry or resentful toward your wife, hold your tongue long enough to take inventory as directed in section 1:

- Recognize that the Bible is true and is the only source of truth that really matters.
- Acknowledge that your name is in the Lamb's Book of Life and that nothing can take us from God's hand.
- Remember that your wife was made specifically by God to be your perfect helper.

Standing on this truth, you are prepared to respond to your wife with a grateful, helpful, and forgiving heart.

If your wife has hurt you, she likely is hurting as well—so comfort her. If she has done something that makes you mad, perhaps she does not understand your expectations—so make the effort to understand her first by asking about her needs in this situation. Then strive to be understood by lovingly instructing her about your needs.

While doing this, tell her you love her and thank her for all that she is. Hold her hand, and be sure she knows you have already forgiven her and hold no grudge against her. Your wife will thrive in this atmosphere of forgiveness.

Seeking counsel

The ideas presented in this book are ones I have developed through years of providing counsel to married couples. Sometimes a couple will try hard to reestablish fellowship and reconcile with one another but just cannot seem to have victory in this area. If that's the case with your marriage, please do not hesitate to seek the help of a good Christian counselor. There is no shame in asking for counsel; as a matter of fact, the Bible tells us it is wise to seek the advice of many counselors (Prov. 15:22).

I do not recommend seeking the advice of everyone around you. Too often, "seeking counsel" turns into finding a few friends who agree with your point of view. Chances are, your divorced or unhappily married coworkers probably won't be helpful in walking you through reconciliation with your wife. My strong suggestion is to seek the help of a person or persons who are called to provide Christian counseling to married couples.

Conclusion

God's objective is always reconciliation; this is why he offered forgiveness of sins to his church. You are called to follow his example and constantly promote and restore fellowship within your family and to others around you. If you practice forgiveness and reconciliation, you will enjoy fellowship.

If you are ever hurt and do not feel that you can provide forgiveness and restoration for fellowship, stop and take inventory. Then forgive as a purposeful act of obedience to God.

Read ... Matthew 5:22–23, in which Jesus tells us that reconciliation through forgiveness is even more important than our acts of worship.

Pray ... Ask God to bring to mind any broken or chipped places in your relationship with your wife.

Write ... a list of any grudges that you are holding against anyone. Then write how you will work toward reconciliation in those situations.

Chapter 16

●◆●

Preseason Scrimmage

*Winning is a habit. Watch your thoughts, they become your
beliefs. Watch your beliefs, they become your words. Watch your
words, they become your actions. Watch your actions, they become
your habits. Watch your habits, they become your character.*

Vince Lombardi

All teams do it: the preseason scrimmage. They practice for a
while first, but before the season of facing opposing teams
starts, they have an intra-team game. At my high school it was
"the Black and White Game," named for our school colors, and it
always took place after we had practiced as a team and worked out
most of our defensive and offensive plays, but before the season
opener. We wanted an opportunity to try what we had learned on
a game field with real referees officiating, the clock ticking, and the
scoreboard lit. There were fans in the stands (mostly our parents,
as well as scouts from other teams) and, of course, cheerleaders to
show off for.

This was also the time to fine-tune anything that did not quite work right. No new plays were tried during the scrimmage; we only ran plays that were well-practiced and ready. In practice a lineman might pose as a ball carrier so others could practice tackling him, but not in the scrimmage: you played your position as if it were a real game.

Scrimmages are meant to be as realistic as possible, so we were told to play hard. I remember a linebacker nicknamed Smiley took this direction so seriously he actually knocked me unconscious when he exploded on a fullback I was trying to tackle.

The red and white scrimmage

With "The Nine Responsibilities of a Husband" as your playbook and your journal as your practice log, you are ready for what I will call "the Red and White Scrimmage." The plays are designed to defeat the enemy and score a happy marriage. Your opponent has been watching your progress and would like nothing better than to see you lose.

Your assignment is to spend time with your wife discussing what you have been reading and learning. Tell her what you are thinking about each play you choose to run, and make sure you get her input, too. Remember, you are asking what she thinks or feels, so there can be no wrong answer and there is no way for that answer to upset or offend you. This is where the scrimmage part comes in. Use the purity of the Word of God (white) in all the plays you run, and then run hard, knowing that all your mistakes are covered by the blood of Christ (red).

The plays

Because a preseason scrimmage is an act of preparation, you may or may not run all the plays you know. The idea is to run a variety of plays, including ones you run well and others you are still working out.

Pick your plays from the list below. You may run all nine, or you may only get around to a few. No matter how many you run, be sure to choose a couple you are comfortable with first, to get into the rhythm of succeeding. Then, pick at least two you need to work on.

- **Play 1: Leader** (Josh. 3:9–11) Are you spending time with God? Do you have a vision for your wife and family? Have you communicated that vision to them?
- **Play 2: Lover** (Gal. 5:22–23) Can your wife see the fruit of the spirit in you? Always? Are you the physical lover she needs?
- **Play 3: Standard Bearer** (Deut. 6:6–9) Are you teaching God's Word to your wife and family, in both word and deed?
- **Play 4: Provider** (Acts 18:7–10) Are you willing to be bold and stand where God has placed you so that you can provide the Gospel message? Are you comfortable in that position?
- **Play 5: Warrior** (James 4:7) Do you stand against evil? Have you seen Satan flee from you?
- **Play 6: Advocate** (Gen. 2:18) Brag about the perfect gift God provided for you. Have you bragged to your wife?
- **Play 7: Intercessor** (Eph. 6:18) Be an intercessor for your wife by praying in the spirit and on all occasions for her. Have you asked your wife how you can pray for her?
- **Play 8: Forgiver** (1 Pet. 4:7–8) Has your love for your wife covered any offenses she may have committed against you? Are you ready to welcome offenders without grumbling?
- **Play 9: Reconciler** (2 Cor. 5:18–19) Have you been deliberate about being an instrument of God's reconciliation?

Conclusion

You have been practicing your responsibilities as a husband; now is the time to practice winning as a husband. As instructed, you should have picked a few plays to run and recorded the results in your journal. How did you do?

Read ... the scriptures from the plays you selected.

Pray ... As you finished this chapter and worked through your plays, there may have been a couple of injuries in the form of hurt feelings. It is important that those injuries are healed, so be sure to conclude with a healing prayer. You might pray something like this:

> *Father,*
> *Thank you for the opportunity to hear your Word and apply it to my life. Thank you for a wife who is a perfect helper. We claim your healing for any hurts that the enemy may have caused during this scrimmage. Satan, you have no authority. We put you on notice right now that this team is ready and will be victorious.*
> *In the mighty name of Jesus,*
> *Amen*

Write ... in your journal:

- the responsibilities you feel good about
- the responsibilities you want to improve
- what your wife is saying about this study

Section 3

• ◆ •

Walking It Out

Practice does not make perfect, it makes permanent.

Larry Hartley

Chapter 17

• ◆ •

Never give up

*Many of life's failures are people who did not realize
how close they were to success when they gave up.*

Thomas A. Edison

In chapter 16 you took time to review each of your responsibilities as a husband and some of the scriptures related to them. The objective was to find those "plays" (responsibilities) that you run well and those you still need to practice. If you fell down or fumbled the ball a few times, it's okay—you are forgiven. Now get up and try again.

Trying again

My wife and I ride our motorcycles every chance we get, even just to run errands around town. Motorcyclists know that there are two kinds of riders: those who have dropped their bikes, and those who will. You just hope no one is watching when you drop yours. I once fell down in the parking lot of the Home Depot. The bike rolled over on its crash bars, and the momentum threw me down on the pavement. I jumped up as quickly as I could so that anyone watching would know that it didn't hurt me because I'm so tough. And, I *was* physically okay (although the fall did hurt my pride a little). The good news (I think) was that I had fallen before, so I knew how to use my knees to right the nine-hundred-pound motorcycle by myself. An observer who had run over to help me commented, "Oh, I see that you've done this before." Thanks for pointing that out, buddy.

He was right, though: I had dropped it before—and that time I needed help to get it back on two wheels. Then the friend who helped me showed me how to pick it up on my own. He explained that he had worked out how to stand one of these beasts up by himself in his garage, by gently laying his bike down and trying different ways until he figured it out.

Jesus says in Luke 11:9 that you are to keep asking and it will be given to you; keep seeking and you will find; and keep knocking and the door will be opened. I say keep trying and you will be a husband who walks out his responsibilities. If you are having trouble being the lover your wife needs, for example, or standing as a warrior against evil, seek help in those areas. Here are some good places to seek help:

- Study the scriptures I've listed in the nine responsibilities. Read them in their broader biblical context to understand them more fully.
- Ask your wife to pray with you about it.
- Look for other publications on the specific subject in question.
- Ask your pastor or another mentor to help you understand and to pray with you.
- Seek out a good friend who will help you and hold you accountable.
- Seek guidance from a Christian counselor.

Seeking help will give you an opportunity to practice acting out your responsibilities correctly. By practicing them correctly, you will develop those skills and not have to "unlearn" any bad habits you might have formed.

Practice makes permanent

I only recently learned that I've been using the front and rear brakes incorrectly when riding my motorcycle slowly. Turns out, I had learned the wrong technique more than twenty years ago. As a result I was unstable and always felt at risk of falling when riding at slow speeds. A good friend gave me a video that explained what I was doing wrong. It showed me a new way of braking, which was definitely more stable but felt very awkward the first time I tried it. To help make this new (and correct) action a habit, I regularly drive to an empty parking lot and turn 180 degrees at a slow speed to the left, then to the right, then left again ... you get the idea. Eventually, through practice, I will make the correct and safe method a permanent habit.

You'd think I would have sought help with my technique the first time I fell down, right? Frankly, I did not know my method was flawed, and I was too proud to ask for help. I just kept practicing the wrong thing, hoping I would get better at it.

I had the same problem with areas of my marriage. Why didn't I seek help the first time I hurt Gay or did not show her I loved her? Or the first time I realized I had spoken to her as if she were my enemy? The reason is simple: like many husbands, I did not know any better. I knew I did not want to keep falling down, but I was too proud to ask for help. Men, as you take up your responsibilities, there may be times you fall down. Resolve right now to swallow your pride and ask for help.

Remove the stumbling blocks

Don't let pride or discouragement get in the way of your trying and trying again. Build on the foundation you have started, and practice doing the inventory and fulfilling your responsibilities until it becomes a natural part of who you are.

There are a few common stumbling blocks which may hinder your ability to live happily ever after with your wife. Each of the following statements will give you spiritual stability as you walk out your responsibilities as a husband:

- *I must decide for my marriage.* If your marriage is a covenant, there is no such thing as a deal-breaker. This is a decision you must make. If you are in your marriage permanently, you will work on living happily ever after. Settle for nothing less than being blissfully happy.

- *My spouse is not my enemy.* No matter what Satan says and no matter who he says it through, your wife is your perfect helper and a gift from God. If you ever feel differently, you are wrong, period. If you think she is the one you have to defeat, you will stumble.

- *My yes is yes, and my no is no.* This concept is so simple, yet we can complicate it so easily! For example, when your wife asks you what you want for dinner, don't say, "Whatever," when you know you won't eat fried fish. Instead say, "Anything but fried fish." If she asks you to do something that you don't want to do, say so. Don't agree to do it and then grumble about it. You said yes, but you didn't mean it. Allowing yourself to be wish-washy about the little things will confuse your efforts in the bigger matters.

- *It is never too late to plant good seed.* Never give up planting good seed in your marriage. I have seen a marriage go from thirty years of terror to blissful happiness in what seemed like no time. Once God is allowed to be in charge and the husband is fulfilling his responsibilities, the harvest of happiness is assured. Keep in mind that Satan will try to convince you that your marriage is not worth investing in because you have tried so long and failed.

The next few chapters are intended to encourage you to make a difference in your marriage daily. Keep working at becoming the leader, lover, standard bearer, provider, warrior, advocate, intercessor, forgiver, and reconciler God has called you to be. If you are married, you have been practicing something already, and that something has become your way of doing and being. You may have practiced those things for thirty years, and now they have become habits. In that case, the only way to change them is to start practicing marriage the way God intended and make his way permanent.

Conclusion

Practice the responsibilities of a husband over and over until you have made them a permanent part of your actions. You may need help from other printed materials, friends, or counselors; be sure to seek help as you walk out your responsibilities.

Remove any stumbling blocks that may be in your way. Decide for your marriage; let your yes be yes and your no be no. Remember that your spouse is not your enemy, Satan is—and that it is never too late to get started on the road to happily ever after.

Read ... Luke 11:5–13. Jesus told us to seek, ask, and knock—and if we keep it up, we will receive the help we need.

Pray ... to remove any stumbling blocks that will hinder you. Pray out loud, making these declarations:

- "I will never leave, no matter what."
- "My wife is not my enemy."
- "My yes is yes, and my no is no."
- "I will continue to plant good seed, and I will reap a harvest of happiness."

Write ... What are you asking God for? Where are you seeking help in your life? What doors are you knocking on?

Chapter 18

◆

The house of bread

I have fond memories of my Grandma Davis baking bread in her little house in Jeffersonville, Indiana. I stayed with her every day one summer when I was about six years old. She would bake a fresh loaf each day, and you could smell it from a block away. So if I was playing outside and smelled fresh bread, I would hurry back to the house to be sure I was there when it came out of the oven. I would have to stand in the kitchen while it cooled enough for her to slice it. After what seemed an eternity, she would pronounce it ready and cut me a generous slice. Before I started eating, I would hold the bread up to my nose for a moment to get a real nose full. The smell alone was so wonderful it almost made me dizzy. Then, finally, I would eat it: no butter, no sugar, no jelly, just Grandma Davis's fresh bread. It was perfect all by itself.

God uses the symbolism of bread often to refer to our need for him. A couple of examples come to mind:

- When Moses set up the tabernacle, God instructed him to have a special table for bread called "showbread." There were twelve loaves to represent the twelve tribes of Israel and God's willingness to fellowship with us.

- When Jesus gave the model for prayer, he instructed us to pray for God to give us our daily bread.

So it is no surprise that Jesus was born in a little town named *Bethlehem*—or "house of bread."

Tim and Opal

The last time I had heard from Tim and Opal, they were doing great. They were reading their Bible and praying together daily, and Opal was feeling safe in a home led by a true provider. But as time went on, Tim began to treat the reading and praying like a chore that needed to be completed, not a time for seeking direction. They reached out to us for help because they felt as though they were slipping into old habits that would lead to another break in their fellowship.

"So how are things going?" I asked.

Opal was quick to compliment her husband on his efforts to present Bible reading in the home. "But it just doesn't seem to mean as much as it did in the beginning," she said.

"That's too bad," I said. "What changed?"

"It's hard to find time to read a proverb, five psalms, our daily devotional, and then spend thirty minutes in prayer," Tim explained. "Some days we cut it short, and other times we just skip it and try to make it up later".

"How does that work out in the long haul?"

"It doesn't. I feel guilty because I think I am shorting my family. But, I also know that sometimes Opal is bored."

Tim and Opal had fallen into the trap of making their daily reading and praying too regimented. It had become a chore to be checked off the list, like making the bed or brushing their teeth, rather than an opportunity to fellowship with God.

Every husband should provide daily fellowship for his family, but it's okay if it looks a little different from day to day. One day you may need to read a whole book of the Bible out loud and spend hours in prayer; another day you may just need to hold your wife's hand and listen to what God is telling you. In Matthew 6:11, Jesus tells us to ask for our daily bread—but he doesn't say what it will look like or exactly where to find it. God wants to meet our daily needs, and how he does that may look different from one day to the next.

Fuel enough for today's bread

When using large masonry ovens to bake bread, a baker needs to understand how much bread he will be baking that day and then stoke the fire accordingly. The bread doesn't bake by the heat of the fire, but by the energy stored in the masonry lining of the oven. Too much fuel or fuel added too quickly will cause that masonry surface to get too hot: the bread will burn on the outside but won't get done enough on the inside, making it inedible. Too little fuel and the oven will not be hot enough for all the bread, which won't bake at all. This makes a sticky mess of hot, ruined dough.

Having the right fellowship with God each day is like putting the right amount of fuel in the oven to bake just enough bread for today. If your family needs a lot of bread to get through the trials of today, spend a little extra time with them to store the heat they will need. Remember, you can put too much heat in the oven and burn the bread, or too little and just have a mess.

Tim and Opal had been trying to use the same amount of fuel for every situation and every day. As a result they were getting bread that was not all that tasty or useful. And if all you get is burned bread or sticky, ruined dough for your efforts, why bother? So they would skip the fellowship for the day and go hungry altogether—or worse, try to live on the poorly baked bread from yesterday. What a mess.

How to add enough fuel

To add the right amount of fuel to the fire, you need to know how much bread will be baked today. You can only know that through an active prayer life and by getting help from your wife. So take time each day to do the following:

- Ask God to bless this day and acknowledge there is nothing you need that God will not provide. I often do this as I am throwing the blanket back and putting my feet on the floor for the first time that day.
- Stop and listen to God. Don't turn on the TV or radio in the morning, but instead spend a few minutes in silence before all the noise of the day begins. The shower can be a great place for this.
- Share with your wife what you are hearing from God. Gay and I make an effort to talk about today's prayer needs before we talk about today. Don't let the news you hear or the troubles you know are coming get in the way.
- Open the Word of God to receive guidance. Be less concerned about the actual amount of reading you do or getting through all of today's devotional reading and more concerned with opening the Word. Read out loud.
- God will speak to you each through the Word. Stop and listen, and then share with each other what you are hearing. Share your praises as well as your prayer needs.
- Pray together. Whenever possible, hold your wife's hand and pray together. Again, don't worry about the length of the prayer—just do it. If you have followed the five steps above, the length of your prayer will be just right.
- Walk in the knowledge that God will bless you this whole day. This is the "follow-through" of the adding fuel exercise.

Follow the points above, and your fire will be just the right temperature and have just the right amount of fuel for a perfectly heated oven—and you will have enough bread for any situation that might pop up today.

Conclusion

Read ... Psalm 23. Consider the promises in this psalm, and use them to guide your prayer, below.

Pray ... for the following, with a thankful heart:

- a lack of nothing (Ps. 23:1–2)
- restoration of your soul (Ps. 23:3)
- guidance toward righteousness, no matter where you are (Ps. 23:4)
- provision, even when the enemy is near (Ps. 23:5)
- goodness and grace all the days of your life (Ps. 23:6)

Write ... What is God telling you about the promises in Psalm 23? What will you teach your family about this psalm?

Chapter 19

◆

Victorious husbands

Robert and Ruth

The voice mail from Robert was urgent—he and Ruth had just had the worst night ever. His message sounded something like this: *You are not going to believe what she did this time. She has lost her mind, and I just don't know what I'm going to do. Call me when you get this.*

We had not met with Robert and Ruth for some time because they were doing fine; the four of us had decided that they did not need to come to weekly sessions anymore. Robert was working his responsibilities as a husband, and Ruth was enjoying the opportunity to brag about her wonderful husband. They seemed well on their way to Happily Ever After.

I did not call Robert back for a couple of days … on purpose. When I did call, this is what happened:

"Hey Robert, I saw that you called. Sorry I was a little slow in getting back with you."

"That's okay, we worked it out."

"Really? What happened?"

Robert explained to me that he had apologized to Ruth for getting upset and had asked her to sit down with him to work out their problem (Forgiver, Reconciler). Robert told Ruth, "I know you are my perfect helper and a gift from God" (Advocate). They spent an hour together discussing where things had gone wrong, and then Robert suggested a plan of action to avoid that pitfall again (Leader).

"I got to pray with her right then, and she loved it," he told me. "That very night I was so in love with her—I think we're going to make it."

Robert had put on the full armor of God and acted on his responsibilities as a husband. As a result, he was victorious against Satan.

I'm not implying that Robert was some sort of saint for doing all this. But it's important to recognize the changes that came about when he began taking care of his responsibilities. He was responding with the ability given to him by God, with Christ as his example and through the power of the Holy Spirit. Ruth still brags about that weekend as a time when she and her husband stood together and fell more deeply in love.

Jim and Sheila

Sheila called to ask if she and Jim could come over right away. It was important, she said, and they needed to see me. I had some open time later that afternoon, and she agreed it could wait that long. So made the appointment.

Promptly at 3:00 p.m., Jim and Sheila showed up.

Jim started talking even before we sat down. "You remember the night I called and was so mad at Sheila?"

"Which one, Jim? You have to be more specific," I said, and we all laughed.

"I was telling you she needed to suck it up, and you were telling me to forgive? Man, I thought you were wrong."

"Interesting," I said. "So was forgiving the wrong answer?"

Turns out forgiveness was exactly what Sheila needed. Because Jim had already forgiven any hurt, they could talk without anger between them. With that groundwork laid, Jim told Sheila that he just needed her to be with him and include him in her plans.

"I had always been sure that Jim would not want to do the things I was planning, so I never invited him," Sheila explained. "Plus, if we weren't doing what he wanted, he would get antsy, so he was no fun anyway."

"I just wanted to be around her," Jim said. "I didn't really care what we were doing."

"He neglected to tell me that, or maybe I stopped listening because he was criticizing me at the same time," Sheila said.

We talked for nearly an hour. They told me the peace in their home was nearly constant, and their daughters had blossomed as a result. Both girls would be going away to college soon.

Jim and Sheila bragged about how deeply in love they were with one another. Sheila was so excited that she jumped up and stood next to Jim, touching his shoulder as she said, "It is just so easy to love a lover and respect a true leader. My man always stands up for me, and it's like I can do no wrong in his eyes; he forgives so easily. Every day he leads us in prayer—not always a long one, but we never miss a day. I love him so much."

I was listening to all this and smiling with them both. *What a great God we serve,* I thought. Jim had been acting out his responsibilities and had taken a leap of faith to boldly face any problems between him and Sheila. As a result, they truly were living happily ever after.

Jim interrupted my daydream. "I have one more thing to show you," he said. "Put on your sunglasses and come outside."

We walked out to the parking area, and there was a great big V-twin motorcycle with enough chrome that, yes, I needed my sunglasses. God is so good. Jim had asked for peace, good children, and a loving wife and received them in abundance. God had also seen fit to provide the beautiful ride I was looking at, just because Jim had been faithful. I watched as Jim hopped on, Sheila climbed on the back, he fired it up, and they rode off together toward Happily Ever After.

Man, I love a happy ending.

Conclusion

What a mighty God we serve. Robert and Jim were not supermen. They were ordinary guys who just wanted to love their wives and live happily ever after. They took God's Word seriously and took up the good work of acting on their responsibilities as husbands.

Read ... your journal entry from day 1. What were your goals on that day?

Pray ... with your wife. Be sure to hold one another and acknowledge her as your teammate. Listen as God sets new goals for your marriage.

Write ... a list of your new goals. If you have a hard time, the following sentence starters might help:

1) The goal for my life is ...
2) The goal for my marriage is ...
3) The goal for my family is ...

Chapter 20

Suit up—it's game day

First I prepare. Then I have faith.

Joe Namath

When I was in high school, dressing for a football game was quite a ceremony. We would take our helmets home the night before and shine them so they would look good under the lights. We would polish our cleats, and coach would give every one of us a new jock and a new pair of socks. Our game jerseys were carefully cleaned and pressed, and we would move our pads from our practice pants to our gold-colored game pants with the black accent stripe down the leg. Once we were dressed, the line coach would inspect us to see if we were ready for the game. If we passed, he would stripe our cheeks with eye black. Man, we looked good.

I was a defensive lineman. My suit-up included forearm and hand pads because I would be putting my hands and arms in places where they would be banged up (I broke most of my fingers multiple times in the four years I played). I did not wear hip pads like the running back, because no one would be trying to tackle me. My shoulder pads were very wide, with all the pads possible, unlike those of the quarterback, who needed more flexibility. Whatever position you played, there was certain equipment you needed in order to be ready to face the opponent.

When we took the field during pregame, we looked like we were there to play, and play to win. It was glorious: the drills were designed to make us look quick, strong, dangerous, and coordinated … they weren't really exercise as much as a dance. We were saying to the opposing team, "Whatever you brought can't possibly defeat us." We had prepared for game day, we were suited up in preparation for victory, and we won—over and over again.

Prepare to take the field, gentlemen, and become the husband God has called you to be. Suit up—it's game day.

The full armor of God

Therefore put on the full armor of God, so that when the day of evil comes, you may be able to stand your ground, and after you have done everything, to stand.

Eph. 6:13

The Bible tells you to stand and to stand firm when you put on your armor, which includes several pieces:

- First, put on your **helmet** of salvation (see chapter 3). This is the helmet that shines under the lights. You need to know you are saved; there can be no question in your mind about this. God himself is the underwriter, and he loves you too much to let it be any other way. Know this!
- Gird your waist with the **belt of truth**. I think of this as a covering for the life-giving parts of your body. Cover them with truth, and plant only the seeds of truth.

- Cover your heart with the **breastplate of righteousness**. A righteous heart will have no trouble leading in the way of the Gospel. It will not judge, and it will be quick to forgive. The man who has a righteous heart will through his prayers provide abundance for his family.

- Always carry the **sword of truth** given to you by the Holy Spirit. And remember, this is a sword, not a pocketknife. Like David cutting the head off Goliath, don't be afraid to cut down evil when you see it.

- Never leave home without your **shield of faith**. Do not underestimate your enemy's ability to hurt you: he will sling everything at you. These days we don't see much in the way of biblical weapons like flaming arrows; usually I am attacked by something more like a setback at work or a bad doctor's report. No matter what form the attacks take, however, they hurt and can slow you down. You need to block them with the faith that God is in charge and on your side. I know Satan doesn't win (I read the end of the book).

- Finally, cover your feet with the **shoes made of the readiness that comes from the Good News of peace**. These are like cleats that dig into the ground and give you sure footing when the enemy tries to push you back. You need spikes to swing a bat hard enough to hit it out of the park, and you will need stability to swing the sword of truth. This is man's work, and we need a sure foundation to do it effectively. The surest foundation of all comes from the peace of knowing the Good News of the Gospel, and knowing it applies to you and your whole household (Acts 16:31).

Pregame warm-up

With your all your armor on, you are ready to take the field. Your warm-up should be designed to put the enemy on notice that you are ready to claim some ground. Say it out loud: "Satan, you have no business in my life, on my property, or near my wife and kids. You must leave now." The Bible tells us that if we resist Satan, he will flee from us (James 4:7).

Next, huddle up and take inventory by reaffirming these statements:

1) Yes, the Bible is true—all the time and in all ways.
2) Yes, I am blood-bought, and nothing Satan does can change that.
3) Yes, I am a husband, and I am here to stay.

Now that you have claimed the field, pray for God's instruction for today's battles, and go out to win.

Win and keep winning

There are a lot of places where we as husbands get an opportunity to win (or lose). Pay attention and you will notice them easily. To win you must stop, think, pray, and make the decision to take a play from Jesus's playbook.

One day I was in a particularly foul mood because a coworker had let me down for the umpteenth time. So I took care of him ... by whispering bad things under my breath about him. As I was driving home—wouldn't you know it—that stupid farmer was driving a harvester down the road and holding me up. And I was already running late because I needed to stop at the grocery to pick up some stuff Gay had forgotten at the store. Once in the store, I picked the checkout line with an idiot clerk who could not figure out how to accept a check from the person in front of me without the manager's help. And of course the manager was busy with "more important" things, so it took her forever to show up. Good thing, because that gave me time to be mad at my wife for being stupid enough to forget stuff and put me here in the first place.

Sounds like a typical bad day, doesn't it? Ever had one? In that one paragraph, I had at least five opportunities to win by stopping my selfish, foul mood and showing the fruit of the spirit:

- I could have interceded for the coworker. Perhaps there was a problem in his life I did not know about that hurt his performance.
- I could have prayed for the farmer's safety as he did a very dangerous job, and perhaps thanked him for feeding me.
- I could have acknowledged that the clerk was doing the best she could and asked for blessings for her and her family.
- I could have trusted the manager's judgment and recognized that perhaps I was not the most important person in the store at that time.
- I could have spent those moments when God had me standing still to pray for my wife and be her advocate with him.

Instead I kept losing each little battle and letting Satan have more and more ground, until finally I allowed him to take ground in my marriage when I decided not to be my wife's advocate. The enemy won five out of five that day. I'll bet I was not all that pleasant to be around when I got home to my wife, either. Sorry, Gay.

I know the examples in this little story seem trivial and the losses inconsequential. Wrong. Any chink in the armor invites another attack. When a team wins, they put one in the win column, regardless of how big the particular battle was. All that matters is that they won. What I know is that winning teams keep winning. I want to win so often that the opposing team doesn't even bother to show up for the game. I, for one, obviously have not arrived at that level of play yet.

Conclusion

You need to be dressed in the full armor of God so that you are ready for whatever the enemy sends against you. Put Satan on notice. Let him know you are not going to allow him a foothold. Tell him you plan to win.

Then go out and win—often and decisively. Make sure you count the wins as wins, and be sure to remind Satan of his losses (he will remind you of yours). Know that if you have accepted Jesus as your personal savior, you are already more than a conqueror (Rom. 8:31, 37).

Read ... Ephesians 6:10–17.

Pray ... for each piece of the armor as you put it on, asking God to show you how each will help you in a specific area of your life. Invite your wife to pray with you.

Write ... about the battles you have won and lost recently. Use this as a time not only to count the wins and losses, but also to inspect the armor. Which weapons worked best? Where are the chinks in your armor that let the enemy win?

Chapter 21

Encouragement and feedback

I firmly believe that any man's finest hour, the greatest fulfillment of all that he holds dear, is that moment when he has worked his heart out in a good cause and lies exhausted on the field of battle—victorious.

Vince Lombardi

When I was a young man, I loved the Packers and thought Vince Lombardi was the greatest. Of course, it did not hurt that he looked a lot like my dad. Phil Bengston's book *Packer Dynasty*, which chronicles the building of the Packers' championship team, describes how Lombardi controlled everything that went on— not because he was mean or needed be in charge, but because he wanted the men who played for him to succeed. He would tell them what to eat and when to sleep, and sometimes even gave them advice about whom to marry. He acted like their father.

Vince Lombardi was there to celebrate when the team won, and he was there with a plan for changes when they did not. He had a strategy and he executed it. He also was a man of God; he was said to stop by church to pray every day on his way to work.

In the end, the players, the fans, the owners, the whole city of Green Bay loved him. They loved him because he loved them enough to have integrity and be the man and the coach they needed.

I don't say all this to hold up Vince Lombardi as your personal role model, but to offer the example of his life as encouragement to you. You are called to have a solid relationship with Christ, to be a man of integrity, and to be the husband your wife needs. You need to have a plan for how you will love your wife, how you will provide for her, and how you will pray for her. You need to be following a road map that will lead your entire family to a relationship with Christ and to peace in your home. I am confident that every husband can achieve this goal and live happily ever after with his wife.

The road to Happily Ever After

Over the last twenty-one days, we have traveled the road to Happily Ever After together. I hope you enjoyed the ride, and I pray that you have arrived here with me, deeper in love and happier for the journey. The road has been paved with your prayers and your efforts to take up your responsibilities as a husband.

The first few chapters describe an exercise I call "taking inventory." I hope that you will use this simple affirmation of truth to overcome any adversity that might arise in your life. A man armed with the knowledge of his salvation, the sword of truth, and the confidence that he will never leave his marriage has already defeated most of the weapons Satan will use to harm him. Get good at reminding yourself of these three things, and watch Satan flee from you (James 4:7).

The next section provides a list of the nine responsibilities of a husband. I can guarantee that if you live up to these responsibilities, you will have a happy wife. And I think we all know that happy wife equals happy life. God will bless you in more ways than you can count when you walk these responsibilities out.

And now you've arrived: welcome to Happily Ever After. Please plan to take up residence here and enjoy the bliss God intended for every married couple. It's my hope that the stories of other successful couples have encouraged you along the way, and that you are ready to add your story to theirs. I pray that you will be fruitful and that your happiness will be multiplied (Gen. 1:28).

I know you can

When I am speaking to a group about something I know is true, I like to say, "I know this like I know my own first name." Usually these are things that I have personally experienced. For example, I know beyond a shadow of a doubt that if you get a fishhook stuck into your scalp up to the barb, it doesn't hurt much—but it's nearly impossible to pull out.[4] While it doesn't take a lot of imagination to understand how I know this, it does take some faith in me as a storyteller to believe it.

However, I can tell you with 100 percent certainty that husbands who have a solid relationship with Christ and apply themselves to walking out their responsibilities will live happily ever after with their wives. I know this like I know my own first name.

So be encouraged. I know you can do this, and I pray you know that, too. Be blessed.

Questions

In conveying ideas you can use on your journey to Happily Ever After, I have tried to present them in a concise and entertaining way—and I may have left some questions unanswered. If you have questions about any of the thoughts, prayers, activities, scriptures,

---

4 Please don't experiment with your or anyone else's scalp to verify my findings.

or concepts presented in this book, please contact me by e-mail at 21days@genesis2-24.net. I would enjoy hearing from you and would love nothing more than to help you live happily ever after.

Feedback

Let me know what you think of this book. I would like to know how the principles taught here have helped your walk as a husband. Feel free to send along any additional pointers that you feel would help other husbands, and please let me know how your own walk is going.

Gay and I welcome your comments about the book: e-mail us at 21days@genesis2-24.net, or leave a comment on our blog at Genesis2-24.net/21days. It is our intention to help others, and your feedback can only make our help that much more effective.

Need help?

The mission of Genesis 2:24 ministries is to return marriage to the honorable place described in God's word. We do this through individual guidance, group teaching, and family events. If you, your church, or your civic organization or club would like to hear more, please contact us. There is never a charge for ministry, because we never will allow funding to be the reason a couple is not happy.

We can be reached via our website, Genesis2-24.net, or by e-mail at info@genesis2-24.net.

Conclusion

You have arrived at Happily Ever After. I am glad you made the journey. One last assignment:

Read ... your journal. Just as you would look over your photos when you get home from vacation, I want you to look back at the last twenty-one days and remember the joy of getting here.

Pray ... Lead your wife, your family, and anyone else who is around in a prayer of thanksgiving for providing you the opportunity to love God and love your wife.

Write ... a proclamation that you will live happily ever after with your wife. Date it—and let Satan know he has lost the battle.

Appendix A:
The Responsibilities of a Husband

◦ ◆ ◦

Leader

As a husband, you are to spend time with God in order to know his vision for you and your family (Exod. 33:7–11). You are to cast a vision for focused action serving God (Josh. 3:9–11). You have final **leadership** responsibility for your family (Josh. 24:15). You are the chief priest (Heb. 6:19–20), and you should **lead** your family to victory through salvation, love, forgiveness, and reconciliation (Luke 19:9–10).

Lover

You are to **love** your wife as God loves you (1 Cor. 13:1–3). That is, you should **love** her unconditionally and like no one else can (Eph. 5:25). You are to prefer her over all things and at all times and in all of your actions (1 John 3:18); you should prefer her in all your words and thoughts (Mal. 2:15). Your wife will observe the fruit of the spirit in your life (Gal. 5:22–23). **Love** her exclusively (Prov. 5:15–19). Be the physical **lover** she needs (Song of Sol. 2:16; 1 Cor. 7:3–5).

Standard Bearer

As a husband, you are to uphold the **standard of holiness** over your home (Exod. 17:15; John 14:23). You are to recognize God as the authority (Matt. 8:5–10). You are called to teach God's Word at all times (Deut. 6:6–9), teaching through your words and deeds (Luke 6:44–45). You are to serve your family and prepare them for a walk with Jesus (John 13:1–7).

Provider

As a husband, you are to **provide** for the physical needs, the spiritual guidance, and the safety of your wife and family (1 Tim. 5:8). You also should **provide** training (1 Tim. 4:16), encouragement, and prayer for your family (Deut. 6:6–9). Your words and deeds must **provide** an example of a life that reflects the Gospel message (Rom. 2:13–14).

Warrior

The **warrior** is not afraid of the enemy, but instead is riled up by him (Deut. 20:2–3). You will battle against the power of darkness in all matters concerning your wife and family (James 4:7; Jude 1:22–23). As the **warrior** husband, listen to your wife when she discerns imminent attack from the enemy (Gen. 2:18). You should always be dressed in the full armor of God, ready to protect your wife and repel the enemy (Eph. 6:11–17).

Advocate

The **advocate** husband is always for his wife and against those who are against her, no matter the circumstances (1 Pet. 3:7). Therefore you will acknowledge her as the perfect gift from God (Gen. 2:18,

23). You are to represent your wife to Father God and at the city gates as without spot or wrinkle (Eph. 5:27).

Intercessor

You should be in constant prayer, thanking God for your wife and **interceding** for her benefit—and praying *for* her, not *about* her (Luke 22:31–32). Pray in the spirit, vigilantly and persistently for her (Eph. 6:18).

Forgiver

Every husband is to be an instrument of God's **forgiveness** (Exod. 34:9). Therefore you must **forgive** always and in all things. You should be the first to reassure your wife that you love her (1 Pet. 4:8) and have **forgiven** her (Matt. 6:14–15); do so even before she offends (Rom. 5:8).

Reconciler

Every husband is to be an instrument of God's **reconciliation** (2 Cor. 5:18–19). You should stand ready to do the work of **reconciliation** (Isa. 6:1–8), modeling it through your actions, and only when necessary through your words (Col. 3:12–13).

Appendix B:
Sample Faith Vision

I developed this faith vision for my wife, Gay, over a period of ten years. I have amended it many times and will continue to do so as God changes our prayer focus. Remember, a faith vision is a form of intercession for your wife; it should be used as a tool to help you focus your prayers for her, not as a list of changes you want her to make.

It should be noted that Gay also has a faith vision for me, which she uses to focus her prayers for my benefit.

My wife is one who knows the will of God for her life, works hard to understand his commands (Exod. 20:1–14) and put them into practice. I praise God in heaven for this gift.

She calls her entire household to obey God and therefore puts them on the path toward life (Prov. 10:17). Thank you, Father, for this perfect helper.

She knows the joy of serving God and that her service brings only joy, because God never mixes blessings and troubles (Prov. 10:22).

She knows that God is the only one who can bring the wonders of her heart's desire to reality (Ps. 72:18). No matter what our house needs, she trusts God to bring it to us. She knows that Zion is where our help comes from.

She is so much a part of me that she is marrow of my bones. I have no blood and no breath that she is not a part of (Gen. 2:23).

She is my best prize here on earth. She is the best gift I ever received. She is my woman, my helper and, the fulfillment of God's promise to complete my household. She is my partner and perfect helpmate. Thank you, God, for thinking enough of me to create her.